Localism, a Philosophy of Government

Mark M. Moore

© copy right 2014

5th edition

The Ridge Enterprise Group

ISBN 978-0692257104

Dedication

This work is dedicated to my children, as part of my struggle to help them grow up in a world that is at least as free as the one I once knew, to my friends who have also struggled for liberty even before a clear understanding of what must be done to win such a struggle became apparent, and to my special anonymous friend, whose keen insights and long discussions with me on the subject have contributed so much to this work.

Table of Contents

Localism and the American Experiment

****

It is difficult to practice a virtue for which one does not have a name. For example, it is hard to be chaste in a culture which has no word for chastity. The same thing applies when the term for a virtue has fallen into disuse, or is far corrupted from its original meaning.

In the same way, it is difficult to work toward a philosophy of government for which one does not have a name, or for which the term has become twisted or corrupted. So it is with the philosophy of government to which I hold. Seeing that there is no current name to describe it; by the grace of God I do bring form and body to this sublime philosophy of human government by giving it a name: Localism.

Localism is the polar opposite of, and deadly enemy to, globalism. It is the friend of nationalism where the aim of national government is to protect the liberties and freedoms of its own citizens, and it is the enemy of nationalism where the aim of the national government is "national greatness." A Localist knows that the greatest nation is not that nation whose war machine is the most terrible, but rather that nation whose people are the most at liberty.

Localism promotes social and community behavior where that philosophy called "socialism" has failed to do so. Localism is superior to libertarianism even in the goal of providing personal liberty. It is conservative in its skepticism of the government's ability to do good if only it were granted vast powers, and classically liberal in its concern for civil rights and respect for a variety of viewpoints.

Localism does not claim to be able to produce a utopia through means of government. Rather it claims to be the best way to protect us from the delusions of madmen who think that utopian visions are even attainable through government action- if only they and their sort were given enough power over our lives of course. Localism does not even guarantee good government. It only guarantees choice of government. It is the free market acting within the framework of choice which will produce good government.

While the philosophy itself has not been given a name or, to my knowledge, spelled out in its entirety as a philosophy before, two specific instances occur in which it has been approximated. Both of them have resulted in some of the best government mankind has ever seen. I refer to the United States from the period of the Articles of Confederation until the start of the civil war, and the Canton system of Switzerland through most of its history.

In both of these cases, approximating localism was a necessity born from the way each of these nations were created from small independent units who were willing to join together in a limited framework. They would only do so on the promise that the unified federal government they were creating would not grow powerful enough to swallow them up and subjugate their interests. In the case of the United States at least, that promise was not kept.

Now might be the time to mention two terms from the American experiment which come closest to Localism. The first term is Federalism. Its meaning has been clouded as a result of the American debate. If it means that there is a central government with powers that are few and defined, and state governments which retain powers that are broad and undefined, then Localism is very much like federalism. Unfortunately the very word "Federal" has come to stand for that central government whose officials deem themselves the final arbiters of all matters great and small.

In the debate surrounding the adoption of the Constitution, the Federalists were the ones who wanted a strong central government, the anti-Federalists opposed it. For them, the Articles of Confederation among the states were enough. The Constitution, especially with addition of the Bill of Rights, contained concessions from the Federalists to those suspicious of a national government. These were meant to bind up the central government and prevent it from coming to dominate the interests and policy making prerogatives of the several states.

In part because of the association in American history of Federalism with those who wanted a stronger central government relative to the anti-federalists, federalism is the wrong term to describe the philosophy of government summed up by localism. Indeed a Localist, while appreciative of the Constitution, would be inclined to believe that history has largely proved the anti-federalists to have been correct.

Localists are not quite "Constitutionalists," though that word comes closer than any other I have found in our political lexicon. It too is a word rarely used, especially by the mass media in this country which are owned by global corporations.

Constitutionalism, like Localism, is an impediment to globalism, and therefore such media are loath to even speak the term. Socialism, Liberalism, and even some stripes of Conservatism, can all be used to advance globalism. In its early phases, which is all we would ever see, even Libertarianism could be used to do so (more on that later). As such, they are all terms which the global media use freely.

It is Constitutionalism and Localism which are incompatible with globalism. It is they which cannot be accommodated within its frame work and it is they which will be deliberately ignored by the media, lest the people find a name under which they can rally to resist global government. For as long as they are unnamed, citizens who oppose globalism will have no positive banner to which they might flock.

The other terms will be bandied back and forth endlessly, keeping citizens divided into one group or the other. The powers care not which group wins, as long as the masses are distracted enough by the struggle so as not to notice the advances of global government and the loss of individual rights-regardless of which of their safe labels rules the day.

Constitutionalism is largely an American construct, and a philosophy of government ought to be more generally applicable. Perhaps Constitutionalism is a subset of localism, or a cousin to it. It all depends of course, on what is in the constitution in question!

In the American view Constitutionalism is simply a philosophy of government in which all types of government should be strictly limited by a

Constitution which is to be interpreted according to the original intent of those who wrote it and ratified it. Its meaning is to be changed only by a laborious amendment process which requires a supermajority over an extended time period.

The original Constitution, until the addition of the 14th and following amendments, was a very localist document. It is less so now, but even in its attenuated form it would, if followed, serve as a significant barrier to the centralization of government power. The decentralization of government (and political) power is the defining tenet of Localism.

Not that it was a perfect document, even then. Contemporaries, especially Jefferson, specifically warned that the Constitution left too many loose ends, particularly in regards as to how to limit the judicial power and the lack of prohibitions on central government partnerships with banking and financial interests.

At this point there are few souls who would consider themselves "Constitutionalists" when asked what political philosophy they hold. Most would say "Conservative", "Moderate", "Liberal" or even

"Libertarian". Even those who actually better fit under the "Constitutionalist" label may claim one of those other labels, simply because the global interests who control the media don't use the Constitutionalist label often.

Because of this, even people who hold in their heads some foggy opinions which would lean that direction don't have a term under which to refine and crystalize them into a competing political philosophy. The result of this practice is to keep the population mentally confined in an artificial left-right paradigm. Yet even among those few who do claim the label constitutionalist, there is confusion about what it must mean, and not all of those ideas are compatible with localism.

For example, many who would call themselves "Constitutionalists" would say that since the 14th amendment was passed, it is within the power of the federal government to be the referee for whether or not laws passed by state or local governments violate the "constitutional rights" of citizens of that locality under the Bill of Rights or other amendments. They cheer when federal courts overturn a state law or local ordinance with which they disagree, and they complain bitterly about "legislating from the bench" when federal courts overturn state laws or local ordinances with which they agree.

What a Constitutionalist ought to say is that the federal courts should recuse themselves from cases where the federal government is not given explicit permission under the Constitution to make rulings. This was the position of the federal courts themselves shortly after the adoption of the 14th amendment. In fact, their ruling in the *Slaughterhouse* case, the first ruling which tested the limits of the 14th, resulted in such a narrow interpretation of the amendment that even an originalist might object to its meager scope.

Since that time the courts have expanded the scope of the amendment to absurd proportions, with the result that they have ruled themselves to be the final authority over virtually every state law and practice. And since their views might vary over time, what state practices are "constitutional" under this warped view varies over time as well.

The truth is that most, but not all, of those ratifying the 14th did not mean for it to authorize the federal courts to selectively apply the Bill of Rights to the states. Certainly it does not say that. Rather the early part of it focuses on due process and equal protection under the law. Here then is a view of the 14th which I believe better accords with the original intent of most of those who ratified the amendment, and is also more compatible with a localist philosophy of government:

The courts were only to, when authorized under a specific law from Congress, make sure legal procedures regarding arrest and conviction were done evenhandedly. They were to insure that even members of the population who were from disfavored groups had the protection of the law for their persons and property.

What the courts were *not* granted under the 14th was the power to rule on whether or not a law passed by a state legislature prohibiting citizens from doing X or Y was "constitutional" or not. They had only the power to make sure that the laws were the same for all adult citizens, and that citizen protections were the same. Thus the federal judiciary could not tell the states "you can't make a law against X" but they could say "those accused of X, even if they are from a disfavored group, are entitled to a jury trial, legal representation..." et cetera.

Over time however, the federal courts granted themselves powers that their forebears considered beyond them. Congress, perhaps secretly pleased at what this outcome meant to the growth of federal power, ignored their oaths and failed to act against this extra-constitutional usurpation. They, officials of the central government, have now made themselves the "referee" of the laws and regulations of every state, city, town and hamlet. They pick which groups they are sympathetic towards, and use them as vehicles to advance their own will.

Let this sink into your head, **the amendments in the Bill of Rights were never meant to be applied to the states. They were restrictions on the federal government only.**

The first amendment, which sets the tone, specifically says that "Congress" shall make no law. States had restrictions on speech, laws against blasphemy, and even state sponsored churches long after the ratification of the bill of rights. Clearly, the founders did not consider these state interventions, which were explicitly prohibited for the federal government under the first amendment, to be any restriction whatsoever upon the states.

This is not to say these are sound polices, and most states eventually adopted state constitutions which impacted these interventions, but my point is that the original intent of the Bill of Rights was to bind the federal government exclusively, not the governments of the states.

How does the third amendment, about the quartering of troops in homes, apply to states which were not even allowed under the constitution to keep troops? How does the seventh, which specifies "Courts of the United States" (i.e. federal courts)? And what of the sixth, which specifies that the accused must be tried in the state and (federal) district in which the crime was committed? These are all written as restrictions on the actions of the federal government because the whole purpose of the Bill of Rights was to bind up the federal government.

Consider that almost all states, even those brought into the union after the Constitution and Bill of

Rights were ratified, had provisions similar to the first, second, and forth amendments in their state constitutions. If the amendments of the Bill of Rights were meant to bind the states, why would states need such provisions in their own constitutions? Clearly, they would not. The original ten amendments to the Constitution were meant to bind the federal government only, not the states.

So the idea that the federal government is the enforcement body for the Bill of Rights against the states turns the original purpose for the Bill of Rights on its head. It perverts it completely. The Bill of Rights was written to give states which were reluctant to adopt a federal constitution (such as North Carolina and Rhode Island) some assurance that the federal government about to be created would be a limited one.

There would have never been a United States had the original states ever thought that the federal government was to sit in the judgment seat of virtually all state laws and practices. The reason for that is simple. Once one accepts the principle that the federal government is in charge of ensuring that states follow the Constitution, as interpreted by its own judges and even in matters of law relating to a state's own citizens, tyranny is assured. All legal power from that point on will accrue to those who control the central government, the only variable is time.

Some Constitutionalists and conservatives believe that the problem of judicial usurpation will be solved by changing the identity of five of the nine Supreme Court Justices. For a Localist, this is a "solution" which does not identify, much less solve, the real problem. The real problem is that so much power is concentrated in so few hands.

The founders would be shocked that the courts have assumed the position of referee over the validity of virtually all laws enacted by elected representatives of democratic majorities throughout all states in the union. No nine persons are wise enough to hold such power. Even if they were ten times wiser than they are, still they would have no right to lord it over the rest of us, and arrange life in our communities to their preferences rather than our own.

Localists propose a more fundamental reversion of government. We go back to the original intent of the founders. Meanwhile, recent disputes between "liberal" and "conservative" factions amount to no more than an argument over who gets to hold the gun that will be pointed at the rest of us. The key tenet of localism is the decentralization of power.

Many of the provisions of the Constitution, and especially the Bill of Rights, were given to satisfy the concerns of men who were localist in governmental philosophy. They were given so that the founders would be coaxed into political union while still retaining most of the advantages of local self-determination. Some of those who wanted a strong central government immediately went to work trying to remove or end-run the barriers erected by the Constitution to protect local determinism. Once we get past the 12th or 13th amendment, virtually every change in the document has had the effect of increasing the centralization of political power.

Where the advocates of tyranny (let us call it what it is, for James Madison noted that the very definition of tyranny is when all power is gathered together in one place) were not able to alter the constitution to centralize power, they ignored it or perverted the meaning of its words. Today we live with a wounded document: ignored, twisted, and to some degree altered away from the purpose for which it was created. It has even been made to be at cross purposes with itself. How can we, for example, square the right of free speech in the first amendment with the command that "the debt of the United States shall not be questioned" in the 14th amendment?

So Constitutionalism is not necessarily the same thing as localism, even though the original Constitution and Bill of Rights were created to address the concerns of men who were localists, if not by name then in their philosophy.

What is Localism?

"An ELECTIVE DESPOTISM was not the government we fought for; but one which should not only be founded on free principles, but in which the powers of government should be so divided and balanced among several bodies of magistracy, as that no one could transcend their legal limits, without being effectually checked and restrained by the others." – James Madison in *"The Federalist Papers #48"*

****

The key tenet of localism is the decentralization of political power. In a world of fallen humans, government is necessary. But if unchecked, government itself becomes the greatest threat to the God-given rights it was established to protect. Government has been defined as that entity which claims monopoly control on the use of force over a given geographic area.

Localism breaks up the monopoly by geographically fractionalizing its reach, and systematically barring every means by which it might grow in power. Government is thereby subjected to the same free market forces which previously, before the rise of the corpo-governmental axis, served us so well.

Rather than attempt to impose one set of rules on all persons, Localism aspires to set free market principles to work so that governments everywhere build the sort of legal structures desired by their populations- and no more. All persons will never agree on the same rules, and under localism they mostly don't have to.

As at the founding of the United States of America, in localism states are co-sovereigns which volunteer to delegate limited amounts of their own power to the central government, not administrative units of the federal government.

Localism takes this voluntary view of political association down to the county, or even lower, level, so that the *transaction costs* of escaping government one dislikes are made so low that the magic of the marketplace punishes government which does not well-serve the people who live under it. Yet it does not merely arrange for government power to be dispersed (we tried that with the Constitution), but is also mindful of how such power might *remain* dispersed.

Localism is built on seven key pillars. Though the vast majority of people do not wish it, power tends to centralize unless measures are in place to prevent it. The goal of these seven principles is to preserve human liberty by blocking every means of centralizing political power:

The Seven Pillars of Localism

1. The central government has only a very limited role in regulating the activity of the co-sovereign states which comprise it. Specifically, it is only authorized to ensure that the co-sovereigns allow for the freedom of federal citizens not individually charged with a crime to leave the co-sovereign and take their property with them. It has no other authority or role in judging the laws or practices of the co-sovereigns as they relate to citizens of the co-sovereign, except that a co-sovereign may

be expelled from the union if the action is initiated by other co-sovereigns.

2. There must be checks and balances not only between the several branches within the central government, but the co-sovereign states, closer to the people, must also have means of checking and balancing the authority of the central government, including any regulatory agencies. In extreme circumstances this must include some form of interposition and nullification, and at great trouble even the means to peacefully separate from a central government which systematically violates the compact which originally bound the member states together.

3. Dispersing governmental power is pointless if political power in still concentrated in the hands of one or two national parties (who are often funded by global interests). The rules for elections should be ordered with an eye to promoting decentralization and choice in the method of determining how candidates are to obtain access to the ballot. Our current rules, in particular the "first past the post" method

to determine winners, artificially imposes a two party system and ought to be scrapped.

4. Learning the lessons of history; we should take the pains to determine where our own Constitution's barriers to prevent centralization of power proved inadequate to the task and decide what additional ones ought to be erected to insure this intent is kept. Areas under this category include (1) judicial usurpation; (2) the abuse/expansion of the ability to regulate interstate commerce; (3) trade agreements and/or environmental treaties; (4) the role of artificial persons called corporations vs. real persons; (5) the character of the standing military; (6) debt and taxes, and most especially; (7) money and the system of banking.

5. Government education will invariably be employed to advance political ends, therefore even this area of government must be localized so that the power to shape young minds and character is dispersed.

6. Co-sovereign power should also have some checks and balances. Even localities within a state should have some agreed on power to

modify punitive laws of the state within their boundaries. Provision should also be made, in egregious cases, for localities to change co-sovereigns.

7. The co-sovereigns (states) themselves should have the sole authority to determine who their citizens are. When the national government alone controls (or fails to control in some cases) immigration and citizenship, it controls the future beliefs, values, and character of the nation.

As I go into depth as to application of the things entailed in these principles you might be tempted to think that government under localist ideas might be overly complicated and messy. Freedom is messy. Making laws with the consent of the governed is far more complicated than making laws from the will of a small elite group. And despite the elaborate ruse of political choice fostered by the elites and their media organs, what we currently have in the west is rule by a relatively small and self-serving elite group.

I believe that you will find that while a central power structure can *make laws* far more efficiently than a decentralized one, it cannot *ensure compliance* and *equity in enforcement* of those laws more efficiently. In fact it is quite the reverse. Governments with centralized power find making laws easy, but must erect huge, costly, messy, and complicated structures to ensure their enforcement. Part of this is inertia, part of it is communications breakdowns inherent in lengthy chains of dissemination, and part of it is that a policy enacted in the distant capitol often has little support amongst the citizens in the heartland.

Pick then your poison. Do you wish to live under a powerful central government where the making of laws is easy and their enforcement difficult-requiring vast apparatuses with complex powers and structures? Or would you prefer one with a decentralized process of lawmaking resulting in much simpler and more localized organs of enforcement? Most people have not ever been presented with the thought that such a trade-off exists, much less that we ought to have the right to choose which we prefer.

Some might object to the provisions which allow for the peaceful alteration of political boundaries should the citizens find their interests would be better served if they severed political bonds with an entity which they considered corrupt, oppressive, and/or incompetent. We must become more attached to freedom, justice and liberty than we are to imaginary lines binding people to power structures which operate against their interests. This can only be obtained by injecting the magic of free markets into the structure of government.

I would also say that some of the concepts I discuss in this volume, some of the messiest, will rarely have to be used. They are safety valves, designed to release pressure in times of extraordinary stress. Their very existence will mitigate the need for their frequent use. Remedies available to the people will serve as a deterrent to those who would conspire for power against our liberties.

Most people prefer stability to turmoil, and constancy to great change. There is a greater danger that they will fail to cease from their own business long enough to pick up these tools to safeguard their liberties than there is danger that they would use them lightly, or without just cause.

The First Pillar: Who Defines Rights?

****

The key tenet of localism is the decentralization of government and political power. By its measure, central government can enforce claims against restrictions on the freedom of movement of citizens enacted by the co-sovereign states which comprise it, but should have no authority to restrict, annul, or declare void any other laws a co-sovereign might choose to make which applies to its own citizens or inhabitants in its own territories.

Freedom of movement has the following components: Except for those incarcerated for a crime or individuals charged with a crime, no co-sovereign shall prevent anyone who wants to leave the co-sovereign to enter another co-sovereign from doing so, nor shall there be any tax, tariff, fee, or other charge to move one's person or property, including title to real property, from one co-sovereign to another. Nor shall there be any outgoing tariffs, taxes, duties, or imposts on goods transported from one co-sovereign into another, though each co-sovereign retains the right to ban the importation of any good.

That's it. Other than laws relating to freedom of movement, the central government should have no power over the laws which a co-sovereign makes regarding its own citizens, or activity which occurs within its own borders. There should be no central government body authorized with evaluating these laws on an individual basis. Should a super-majority of co-sovereigns find the duly enacted laws of another co-sovereign to be unbearable, the proper course of action is to expel that member from the nation, not send in people with guns to impose a position which is opposed by a clear majority of the co-sovereign's citizens.

Localism ends the national struggle over "who gets to hold the gun" to be pointed at the rest of us to make us behave as they wish. Each state or co-sovereign gets to hold its own gun, but as you will see as you read on, if this power is abused by a state they might find there is simply no one left under their authority to point it at. Both individual citizens and even whole counties would leave their jurisdiction. So, there is no one gun in localism, even to the extent any gun is needed in a society where rules are made locally and reflect the wishes of the local population.

If some citizen of that state does not like the laws imposed by the majority of electors in that state, then they are free to leave and take their goods with them to a locality whose rules are more to their liking. Or if their neighbors also agree with them, they might jointly take measures we will discuss later to either modify the sanctions or take their locality out from under the burden of those laws.

Thus New York and California do not have to fight with the South over whose morality is imposed on the whole of the nation. Nobody's morality is imposed on the whole nation. Each co-sovereign gets to set the bar where its own citizens see fit, and anyone who dislikes that setting can either fight it out to reset the bar, or go to a place where the predominant views fit better with their own.

For those who can't bear the thought that a co-sovereign government in a distant state is not treating some citizen who volunteers to stay there of their own free will as you think they ought, remember that the only other choice is to hand all power to judge what laws are right or wrong to a few people in a single city. Such concentrated power will corrupt into tyranny, as we have begun to see with our own eyes.

Some may be shocked by the paradox that the best way to protect civil rights is to greatly limit the role of the central government in enforcing them. The truth is that interjecting more free market into government, where governments must compete with one another to attract citizens and abusive government is very easy to escape from, will preserve liberty and prosperity much better than granting the central government a near infinite amount of power to "protect rights."

We observe that when a central government obtains such power, it becomes an attractive target for various factions, all of whom wish to seize the machinery of state in order to impose their special view of "rights" on the rest of the population. They use the pretext of protecting the invented "rights" of some sliver of the population as a lever by which they separate self-government from the people.

This arrangement almost begs for a transition in judicial thought from the idea that "civil rights" are individual claims (as individuals) against the government, to the corrosive concept of group-based "civil rights" of one class of private citizens against another class. This devolves into nothing more than political power grabs by one government-favored coalition of citizens against other less favored groups of citizens.

When civil rights are ascribed to individuals, it is government which is the target of claims that rights have been violated. It is government which is restrained by a proper civil rights-claim. When such rights are (illegitimately) assigned to groups, government becomes the referee between competing groups, and it is disfavored groups which are targeted by rights-claims. Government then uses group rights-claims to pit one segment of society against another. It is then the citizens which are restrained by civil rights-claims, not government!

What was originally meant to protect individuals from government action is turned round to be the stick government uses to force people into favored collectives for protection from other groups which use government to loot or oppresses either individuals or those from losing coalitions. Those who control the media and the system pick which groups are favored and which groups are disfavored on any given day, so that there is no security of rights in this arrangement, only a constant need to suck up to those who controls the "rights-making" machinery.

This is not to say that rights don't exist and ought to be protected even if a person is a minority within their locality. Such rights definitely do exist. Localism is not communitarianism. Rather, it is meant to operate within a collection of Republics. By "Republic" we mean a form of government where the powers of government are limited by a founding document and certain recognized rights of individual citizens are not subject to majority vote. These rights however, are individual rights, not group rights which force people into some collective to access them, ultimately undermining the individual.

The co-sovereigns are morally bound (and presumably bound by their own constitutions) to respect citizen's rights, but no single central authority would be the sole basis for determining the outer boundaries of such rights for the whole of the nation. Even in this, it is the market, it is competition not unitary monopolization, which will produce excellence and maximize individual freedom. This will be expressed in the increased power to vote with one's feet, the free market competition for citizens, the remedies possessed by local governments against the co-sovereigns under localism, and the fear of expulsion from the nation.

We should also note that the central government, when it objects to the practices of a co-sovereign, is limited to objecting to actions of *agents of the co-sovereign government*. It should have no authority whatsoever to arrest state citizens who are not acting under the color of government authority. That is the state's purview.

In the localist ideal the state should serve as an intermediary protecting its citizens from direct federal police action. However, should the state fail to act against those preventing the free movement of federal citizens residing in a state, the federal government would be justified in moving against state agents (official or de-facto) who were complicit in restricting or deliberately failing to protect legitimate freedom of movement.

For those who fear this solution falls short of perfection, I urge you not to compare it to perfection. Perfection is not an attainable goal of human government and people who believe that it is are dangerous. Rather compare it to the two alternatives. The other possibilities are a nation where everyone is constrained to think and act alike by the central government, or conflict and division as first one faction and then another gains control of the central machinery which overrides the people's right to self-government in the name of protecting what are often pseudo-rights.

The Second Pillar: Remedies against Injustice by Central Governments

"The spirit of encroachment tends to consolidate the powers of all the departments in one, and thus to create, whatever the form of government, a real despotism. A just estimate of that love of power, and proneness to abuse it, which predominates in the human heart is sufficient to satisfy us of the truth of this position." – George Washington in His Farewell Address, September 17th, 1796

****

What good are paper protections from federal government violations of our liberties if those alleged protections are not paired with remedies? Protections on paper alone are inadequate to safeguard the liberties of the people from an over-reaching central government. Unspecified remedies for violation of the compact become illusory remedies.

This is most especially true when the central government maintains the fiction that the power to interpret the meaning of those words and protections ought to be stripped from the people, their state courts, and their state legislatures and reserved exclusively to a select few members of their own caste.

Though guarantees and assurances might be spelled out in writing, there is not one person reading this document who would be so foolish as to sign an important compact with another if they believed that only the other party to the compact had the authority to decide when they were keeping it and when you were keeping it. Who then can seriously maintain that the Founders assigned exclusively to the federal government the power to determine whether or not that government was staying inside the limitations laid out for it in the Constitution?

The Founders clearly understood that the states which made the compact establishing the central government retained the power to determine when that government exceeded the grant of powers issued in the compact. James Madison said as much in the Virginia Resolution, and Thomas Jefferson echoed a similar principle in the Kentucky resolution.

So first we must understand that the central government does not have exclusive jurisdiction to determine the limits of its own powers. That is madness. Once we understand this, we might turn our attention to what redress might be available to the co-sovereigns when faced with acts of a central government which exceed the authority granted it in the compact which established the relationship. In the case of the United States, this would be the Constitution.

Let's next then consider what a co-sovereign might do if it found the central government was exceeding its authority under the terms of the compact by which it was established....

Interposition and Nullification

This is not meant to be anything like a complete treatise on the history or even the issue of Interposition and Nullification. For those not familiar with those terms, they come from the Virginia Resolution and the Kentucky Resolution, authored by James Madison and Thomas Jefferson respectively. Though Madison in later years somewhat crab-walked away from the position expressed in the Virginia Resolution, when speaking of it I will refer to the position on the matter he held whilst under federal power, rather than that expressed after he wielded it.

The principle of Interposition postulates that it is the states which are ultimately in charge of determining when the federal government has exceeded its authority under the constitution, rather than some employee of that same government, such as the judges of the federal courts. When a state determines that the federal government is exceeding its authority in some way which harms the citizens of that state, the state is "duty bound" (to quote the Virginia resolution) to interpose itself between the federal government and those citizens whose rights are being violated.

The principle of Nullification is similar. It specifies that encroachment of rights left to the states or to the people by the federal government justifies the state defending the rights of both. It also says that one remedy available is for the state to declare the encroaching federal law or policy of no effect on the soil of that state.

In both concepts, the state has only the right to take action against federal law or policy which is beyond the authority allowed it in the constitution, not for any law or policy which it dislikes. The action might take various forms, from simply urging passage of a constitutional amendment with stronger language specifically barring the federal government from certain acts, to arresting federal agents who attempt to use force against a state's citizens in the course of implementing the federal policy or law. The spectrum of possible responses is broad.

Under localist arrangements, the more drastic forms of nullification or interposition would seldom or never need to be used. The federal government would have little opportunity or means to violate the rights of the co-sovereigns or its citizens, and if the matter went to court the judges would not be from the federal government, but from the other states (more on that under the fourth pillar).

Still, ultimately there are only two possible answers to the question of self-determination: a co-sovereign can determine when the rights of its citizens are being violated by the federal government or it must leave that determination to others. Either the co-sovereigns may determine when the federal government is exceeding the legitimate authority granted to it by the states, or they must leave that determination to the federal government itself.

A Localist would of course favor some method of interposition or nullification at least as an option, especially in a situation such as the one we are now in. Currently we see that the safeguards against federal encroachment are few, and lifetime employees of the federal government itself claim the ultimate authority to determine the limits of their employer's power. If we leave it at that, we should not be surprised to find that over time they determine that the central government should have virtually all power.

One would hope that matters could be resolved peacefully, and with principled compromise. Indeed in a localist country, they would always be resolved peaceably, because a state dissatisfied enough with federal policy would have a process by which they could peacefully leave the union. The potential for violence comes from our present system, where limits that seem clear in the Constitution are ignored by a federal government which claims a monopoly right to determine what the words in the compact (i.e. the Constitution) between it and the states may mean.

The position of Madison and Jefferson, as expressed in the resolutions, argue that the two parties to a compact (in this case a state and the federal government) *each* have the authority to determine when the other party is violating it.

Intermediate levels of interposition and nullification might be for states to pass laws forbidding any of its employees or officers to aid the federal government in the implementation of a law it felt was a violation of the compact. It might impose special taxes, fines, or other sanctions, on suppliers within the state for assisting in the implementation of a federal program that violated the constitution. It might impose its own safety and security requirements on such operations- regulating the would-be regulators.

There are various things states can do to resist unjust federal laws which stop short of violence. Enforcing edicts which come from a distant capitol out in the hinterlands is difficult to do without the cooperation of officials in those hinterlands. It's hard anyway, due to shear inertia. Add a little more resistance, and the machinery of oppression can seize up, or at least experience so much wear and tear that compromise is sought out.

On Expulsion and Secession

But of course states are not perfect either. What might happen in a localist nation if a co-sovereign behaves abominably in the eyes of most of the nation and thumbs its nose at the rest of the country? Do we send in people with guns and force them to do it the way those who control the central government want it done (even though about 40% of the population in most states might happen to agree with the offending co-sovereign)? That's the "control freak" solution advocated by proponents of empire. Those dedicated to a Republic might argue, if compromise absolutely cannot be reached, for peaceful expulsion of an intransigent state.

Presumably remaining in the nation will be a benefit to the inhabitants of a state, one that they will not wish to lose. If remaining joined to a nation is not seen as a benefit, then perhaps that nation has a bigger problem than a wayward state. No one wants to be voted off the island while the island offers advantage. A state which errs might risk being kicked out by a super-majority of the co-sovereigns.

It should be the co-sovereigns themselves which initiate this move. The central government should only have the power to ratify it or not ratify it. The threat of disassociation, rather than armed invasion, ought to be enough to hold a nation together, providing its national government is truly offering something of value to the citizens.

I suspect this route will rarely be used. It is those who love to accumulate power over others that are the greatest threat to liberty. Such people are ever willing to use violence to expand the territories over which they might exercise power, using whatever fig leaf of moral justification they might find. Those same personalities will be extremely reluctant to vote to cast away even limited claims of power over a co-sovereign through the vehicle of expulsion.

Though it may be easy for them to vote to kill in order to expand their power, I predict it will be excruciatingly difficult for them to vote to peacefully separate from the smallest shred of it by expelling a troublesome co-sovereign. Expulsion is a tool that will rarely be used, and when used will be preferable to the violence and oppression that is the other option.

Since decentralization of power is the central tenet of localism, it only stands to reason if there is a procedure to remove a member state from the union by the other members and the central government, there must also be a procedure by which a member who wishes to leave the union and take back the authority it once delegated to the general government may do so. Relationships should ultimately be voluntary, not a matter of coercion.

I would suggest that the procedure for a member state to dissolve its bond with the union be spelled out in advance. There ought be two paths to leave, either a super-majority of the population approves a measure in a way that takes a relatively short period of time or a simple majority can approve it in a way that takes a long period of time, such as a decade. The details might vary among the co-sovereigns.

Deciding in advance on what the rules would be for an exit establishes the principle that an exit is an option and could save a lot of needless conflict later on. Many states who joined the American Union thought that since there was no mention in the Constitution of the Federal government being granted the power to force states to remain in the Union, that each state retained the power to leave anytime they chose. They found out the hard way that some things in a contract should be spelled out in advance, such as how each party may terminate the agreement.

The Third Pillar: On Political Parties

"However [political parties] may now and then answer popular ends, they are likely in the course of time and things, to become potent engines, by which cunning, ambitious, and unprincipled men will be enabled to subvert the power of the people and to usurp for themselves the reins of government...."

George Washington from his farewell address

****

The key tenet of localism is the decentralization of government power. Unfortunately, national political parties represent a deforming and centralizing force which can quickly short-circuit self-government. Regardless of how you may feel on the individual issues, citizens against globalization in all its forms have no party to advocate for them.

This claim applies to trade or environmental agreements which weaken national sovereignty, immigration policies which globalize the labor pool, military policies advocating global interventions, financial policies promoting taxpayer rescue of global banks, and so on. The differences in the two established political parties have become meaningless. They both advocate big government (ultimately global) solutions to all social, economic, foreign relations, and monetary issues.

The reason for this is that they themselves represent a centralization of political power, the very opposite of the key tenet of localism. Discontent has never been higher, yet these policies are pursued at flank speed regardless.

Starry-eyed reformers enter the current system with ideas of "taking back" one of the two main parties. With rare exceptions, they don't get very far or rise very high with their idealism intact. Jesus Christ said that "No man can serve two masters." I don't believe that He was mistaken. The candidates we elect cannot serve both their party and their constituents. Those two often have very different interests.

In this system, the most successful politician is the one with the sociopathic ability to appear to their constituents to be fighting for their interests, but in reality doing what is necessary to please a party hierarchy.

That party hierarchy lives on special interest money that is largely global rather than national in character. The two party system serves global elites well, but is hopelessly corrupted for the purpose of providing candidates who will serve the interests of the citizens. Ergo, we need a more just and decentralized system.

The two-party system survives only because it is propped up by election laws designed for that purpose. Have you ever wondered why our general elections for important offices use a "first past the post" method of selecting a winner as opposed to some sort of run-off? When the two parties select their own nominees, they don't normally use the "first past the post" method to determine the winner. They have primary run-offs. Nor do they use the method they have imposed on the rest of us to elect their own party Chairman and officers. They have run-offs.

There are run-offs for local elections in most states. In the general election for higher offices however, the person with the most votes, even if well short of the majority, "wins" the election. Have you ever wondered who benefits from such an odd method of determining the winner?

The answer is the two dominant political parties, and their financial masters. They benefit at the voter's expense. The "first past the post" method frightens people into voting for "the lessor of two evils" rather than permitting them to vote their conscience. Even if voters feel like a third party or independent candidate would serve them better, they are frightened into voting for the candidates of one of the two established parties out of fear that "splitting the vote" would elect their least-preferred choice.

Thus it is that campaigns become disgusting mud-fests. Two parties which are not serving citizens well send us candidates with nothing left to offer except trying to hit your fear button. They don't have to inspire voters, just convince them that they are not quite as loathsome as the alternative.

The solution is to liberate the voters by correcting the flaw which was intentionally inserted in the election system to confine them. The "first past the post" method of determining winners should be abolished. A localist will support run-off elections for all offices, preferably instant run-off elections, in order to maximize participation.

Instant run-off, or "Ranked Choice Voting" is the best solution. It will be vehemently opposed by politicians who serve their party rather than their constituents. I would encourage readers to do a web search and read up on instant run-off voting. Suffice to say that a localist will support some sort of run-off elections for all offices in the general election, not just the primaries.

Speaking of primaries, the current primary process we have for selecting candidates is not a part of the constitution or the intent of the Founders. The primary elections we have now are a rather recent development put in by the two parties after they gained power. You may not be surprised to read that the effect of these rules is to help them keep that power.

In our current system, parties benefit from collecting candidate filing fees, but citizens pay for party primary elections. Why should parties be entitled to taxpayer funded primaries at all? This must result in some sort of injustice. If the primaries are "closed" to individuals not affiliated with their party then the result is the injustice of a citizen being taxed to finance an election for a private organization in which that citizen has no vote.

If primaries are "open" then we will see increasing instances of what we have recently observed in American elections. The insiders in both parties have rescued incumbents who have riled their base by strategically sending their voting blocks to "cross-vote." When the establishments of both parties are willing to cover for each other's "team players" in this manner, the grassroots of each party have a harder time effecting real change.

In addition, open primaries grant a large advantage to whichever party ruthlessly suppresses intra-party competition and dissent within its ranks. If one party has very few seriously contested primaries and the other party has many, then supporters of the first party can "cross-over" and sabotage the primary of the other party by deliberately voting for the worst candidates.

The current arrangement, where private parties collect candidate filing fees but taxpayers as a whole finance primary elections, is designed to subsidize and legitimize these two private organizations as the "normal" means of obtaining access to the ballot. The just and healthy thing to do would be to end the subsidy. I favor ending the free publicity of these primary campaigns and allow all parties to nominate by caucus.

The parties should nominate by caucus. One advantage of this for members of a party is that outside blocks of voters would not be able to pick their candidates for them. Also, the larger population would better understand that these organizations are private clubs, not something enshrined in our constitution or the "normal" way to do things. The present voting method only appears normal because once the parties became established they changed the laws to make it seem so.

Some people, like Former Minnesota Governor Jesse Ventura, have called for abolishing political parties altogether, demoting them to the status of political action committees. Candidates would run with their support, but not under their label. Ballot access would be obtained by gathering a modest number of voter signatures. The run-off system would sort out the choices.

While Ventura may go too far, it is clear that a unitary national political party system which controls candidate's access to the ballot at all levels of government will work at cross-purposes with not only localist ideas, but even the very principle of separation of powers on which the American government was established. Instead of state officials and officials of the central government serving as a check and balance on one another, the national unitary party system makes them co-conspirators in the same club.

Many Americans want the states to be more assertive in maintaining their powers and prerogatives from encroachment by the central government. Localists are among them. But one must see that so long as state office holders are members of the same political club as federal office holders that any claims by politicians to be working toward this goal can only be a charade. Separation of powers is undermined by unity of political hierarchy.

In the same way, our present party system makes the concept of a legislative branch of government superfluous. If the President or Governor, the Chief Executive, is of a legislator's party then that legislator needs no constituents. Rather, they get his or her agenda from the head of their party. And if they are of the opposite party, why then they still have a Speaker or Whip or Leader or some other such figure to answer to who is not and never will live in said legislator's district.

Regardless of who is in the majority legislatively, in the current party system about half of any legislators will be in the same party or coalition as the executive. There will be little legislative oversight from them. They will ferociously cover for the executive of their party and his or her minions. They will support their initiatives. This leads to increased executive power at the expense of the legislative. We can either have the system of Checks and Balances intended by the Founders or we can have the present national unitary political party system. Since the latter undermines the former, we cannot have both.

We must face facts squarely. The reason so many people feel that their Congressman does not represent them anymore is because they don't. The party system has destroyed the functioning of the legislative branch of government as intended by the Founders. What was meant to be the branch of government that was closest to the people and a "first among equals" has become the least powerful branch of government. The unitary party system has ruined representative government.

The party system has turned what was meant to be a healthy tension between the states and the central government into an unhealthy fusion of political power. The unified party system has also turned what was meant to be a healthy tension between the executive branch and the legislative branch into an unhealthy fusion of power. In short, it has undermined the purpose of having a legislature.

Let me also mention here a related reason that Congress no longer represents their constituents: the dilution of representation. When our nation was first founded, each congressman represented less than 50,000 citizens. Now each congressman "represents" over 700,000 of them.

Because of this congressman are harder to reach, and harder to beat, but easier to buy off and control from a central point relative to their position early in our nation's history. A localist would support increasing the number of representatives in order to increase the representation of each citizen. This would reverse the 1929 law artificially limiting it to 435 members no matter how large the population. The same principle applies to state legislatures.

Who benefited from the decision to limit the number of Congressmen? The two parties benefit from making the offices they control access to rarer and dearer and harder to obtain by grassroots means alone. The people benefit when they have more representation and their elected officials can be turned out with a smaller-scale grassroots effort.

Still, political parties are a natural result of people with like views banding together for the purpose of advancing their interests. There is nothing inherently wrong with that. Many well-meaning people want political parties, just not ones which are controlled by special interests in a distant capitol- or even funded by corporations whose interests are global rather than attached to those of the nation.

The reason political parties as they currently exist undermine the intent of the Founders is that they are centralized. In order for political parties to do good and no harm, they must be decentralized. This refers to both state versus federal issues and legislative vs. executive issues.

The most fundamentally important change that should be made in regards to the law concerning political parties is that states should ban by law political parties who field candidates for state and local offices from running candidates for federal office. Likewise, parties which run candidates for federal offices should be banned from running candidates for state and local offices. Without such a firewall, the formal checks and balances between state governments and the federal government will become nullified by informal means.

The states and the central government were meant to be a check and balance upon one another, but the founder's intent in this matter is undermined when all officials from city councilman to President can be members of the same political party, moving up the same hierarchy, and funded by the same people.

This leaves the issue of making sure parties do not continue to serve as an end-run on the intended division of power between the executive branch and the legislative branch. Because legislative seats are much nearer to the people, and on the state level at least so much more within reach of a grassroots effort, an outright ban on parties running candidates for both branches may not be needed. That is, they may not be needed provided that ballot access laws are such that citizens can be elected to the legislative branch via numerous potential sources.

If only a quarter or less of the legislature is of the same party as the chief executive, the abuses associated with having both emerge from the same political machinery are greatly attenuated. Perhaps ballot access laws ought be liberalized to the point where many parties are represented in the legislature. Such laws could even allow for regional groups within a state to recruit candidates only for legislative seats in that region. Better still would be if many legislative seats would be filled by independents who owe only the people in their district and not any party machinery at all.

More on that in a bit, but first let me mention several other ideas which are necessary to keep the new and decentralized state political parties which would be formed under localist ideas truly free and independent from the influences which have so captured and corrupted the current system.

It would be wise to take the step of banning donations to state political parties and PACS not only from corporations, but also from persons or PACS who do not reside in the state in which the party is headquartered. Individuals from other states could still contribute to individual candidates, but candidates could not take money from political parties headquartered in other states, except for candidates for the federal executive.

Certainly corporate donations should be banned. Corporations are not real persons with God-given rights. They are artificial legal constructs which unfortunately have gained more access to our elected leaders than real citizens have.

Since ownership of corporations is spread among citizens of the world, they should not be able to help determine the outcome of elections within a particular nation. The only exception would be a corporation formed specifically for the purpose of political action, a PAC, whose members were composed entirely of citizens.

The goal of all of these barriers is to make sure the political power inherent in a political party is divided so that it is extremely difficult to consolidate such power away from the local people on the ground and move it away to a central location. Should such consolidation occur, these rules make it much easier for citizens on the ground to take the power back. In such an arrangement it would be harder for the centralizers to gain control of the political, and easier for the non-political-professionals (i.e. the people) to take them back should the centralizers ever seize them.

Just as we believe decentralization of government power will bring the magic of the free market to government on a geographic basis, decentralizing the power of the political party will bring the magic of the free market to political action. It is absurd that Americans have a wide array of market choices for almost every product and service in their lives except for political representation. The system has been rigged to try and force all "choice" into one of two parties which at any rate don't disagree on many key issues. The reforms suggested here will break the duopoly which, like almost all monopolies or duopolies, does not serve the public well.

While these reforms do not ban political parties, it is easy to see that the present system is set up to maximize their importance while in order to protect the integrity of our system of government they should be minimized. This reduction in the importance of political parties can only accrue to the benefit of the nation and its people. This blessing upon the citizens will manifest as a disaster to the lobbyists, the professional operatives, hacks, and various other parasites which seek out centers of power in order to obtain personal enrichment out of proportion to their talents and contributions to society.

Ultimately the decentralization of parties will make them superfluous for many offices. The best thing that could happen would be that independent candidates, who count on their good name and life of virtue rather than a party label, would seek to serve in a local or district office (where most of the real authority is in localism) with the backing of citizens groups. This groups would help the candidate, but not control them. The candidate would not run under their label, but only with their endorsement.

These citizen's groups would be autonomous political organizations which help candidates gather signatures for ballot access, but the candidates would stand or fall on their own name and ultimately owe allegiance only to the voters in his or her district of service, not a party machine or party label. Wouldn't that be a welcome switch?

Most of this work does not have immediate practical application, or "action points." This section is the exception. We may not have the opportunity to rebuild a flawed and corrupted framework for government in the near future, but we can get to work building a rival to the flawed and corrupted centralized two-party system right now.

Even today people could join together with other activists in the region of the state where they live and form an autonomous political organization which recruits and backs good independent candidates for local offices. That is where change starts.

Replace the parties locally, so that you will at least have local candidates who are listening to you and don't owe their position to an alien organization headquartered in a distant capitol and funded by global interests. In elections for local offices, party labels don't mean as much as finding a candidate with a good name, especially in small towns. Nor does it take a million dollars in campaign contributions to be competitive in such races. I would advise you to begin today.

The Fourth Pillar: The Lessons of History

"The disadvantage of men not knowing the past is that they do not know the present. History is a hill or high point of vantage, from which alone men see the town in which they live or the age in which they are living." - G. K. Chesterton

****

In a structure supported by seven pillars, it is the fourth pillar which is central to the entire edifice. So it is here. The foundation on which we build is the finest document of government which mankind has devised, the Constitution of the United States. If time reveals cracks in the structure, we ought not be amazed. Instead we should reverently consider how well our current Constitution has worked and is still working to preserve human liberty in the face of all who scheme against it. Liberty is not the typical human condition.

This fourth pillar of the seven consists of seven sections or areas where the history of the American experience has shown us that the provisions of the Constitution were, though correct in their intentions, inadequate to safeguard the localist views of the Founders from the creeping centralization of government power.

The First Lesson of History: On the National Judiciary

Suppose we were able to build a nation from scratch on localist principles. The national judicial power would have very limited authority to rule on cases arising from laws of co-sovereigns as they apply to their own citizens. Such authority would be restricted to cases relating to freedom of movement.

Yet there will still be circumstances where a national judiciary is needed. Some cases will arise from the limited number of national laws allowed. There may be controversies between two or more co-sovereigns. A national judicial body will be required, yet history shows us that such bodies must be checked and balanced lest they usurp ever more power to themselves.

Since the safe guards which the founders provided against judicial usurpation have been shown to be grossly inadequate, it is necessary to go beyond them. The balance was tipped against the states early in our history, even while Judges were still being confirmed by Senators who were selected by state legislatures.

Certainly that safeguard of confirmation by a body which represents the interests of the states ought to be returned. It could easily be done without the need to alter the federal constitution. States could simply have nominations for the federal senate come through the state legislature rather than through a primary. The citizens would then elect whichever nominee they choose in the general election.

There are two other powers the legislature has against the judicial branch, and though rarely used they ought to be retained. The ability of the national legislature to define and limit the authority of the national court ought to be retained. The ability of the national legislature to impeach judges ought to be retained, though Jefferson derided it as not even a scarecrow.

But the above measures would merely restore and sustain the checks and balances against federal encroachment via the judiciary which I have already noted have been shown to be inadequate. What might be added to them in order to bring true form and life to a barrier against federal encroachment of state prerogatives by means of the federal judiciary?

I propose that in the matter of a controversy between a co-sovereign and the federal government, the issue be decided by rotating panels of judges drawn from among the state supreme courts or other distinguished judges: These judges to preside for a period of two years or less and then to return to the states and a new panel assembled.

A random drawing could determine from which state the jurists are drawn, except that states which had someone serve in the previous drawing would be excluded from the current one. The Governor of the co-sovereign state would then appoint the jurist from his state. And of course, if a state from which a judge is a resident is a party to a case with the federal government then that judge could recuse themselves.

This completely shifts the balance of power. Instead of federal judges determining how much power the Federal government ought to have over the co-sovereign states, judges from states who are not a party to the controversy make the ruling. Federal judges have an unfortunate tendency to favor federal power, and indeed have a conflict of interest. Their employer is a party to the case. A localist solution of drawing jurists for such cases from states not a party to the controversy would not permit such a conflict.

For the Supreme Court which hears all other cases where the Federal government is involved, they should be confirmed by a legislative body appointed by the states, as was the case with the U.S. Senate until 1913. They should also be drawn from a limited pool. Instead of the federal executive being able to nominate anyone they please, the Chief Executive of each Sovereign should have the right to make a nomination, and the Federal executive must select from among those nominated to send for confirmation.

Federal judges would still have the power of judicial review of federal laws, just as state judges would retain it regarding state laws. Judicial review is an important safeguard to liberty, but the power as properly exercised is a restraint on the executive branch. Recently judicial review has been abused to expand its purview.

A Second Lesson: On Commerce and Environmental Laws and Treaties

The key tenet of localism is the decentralization of government power. In terms of trade government power can take two forms; power to make trade between political units more attractive to the consumer and power to make it less attractive. Government power can be used either way. In the former category are managed trade agreements (often deceptively named "free trade agreements") and government subsidies of favorite industries. In the latter category are tariffs, import bans, and the like. Either method of government interference in free trade is unfortunate in that it makes that trade less free.

Let's start with trade agreements between national governments. The tendency of late is to make them multi-party. This trend cannot but transfer power to a group outside the sovereignty of each party. Once we agree to terms with ten other nations, who resolves conflicts between those nations regarding whether or not they are living up to the agreement and what they ought to have to do to live up to it? The answer can only be some international body. We have seen an increasing tendency for our government to transfer sovereign authority to transnational groups via treaty.

Because of this, a nation whose charter is localist in nature should ban all multiparty trade agreements. The national government should be prohibited from entering into such an agreement because it cannot do so without transferring some of its sovereignty to an international body. International or global government is the exact opposite of the key tenet of the localist philosophy.

Bilateral trade is a different matter. In bilateral trade, there is only one other party to the agreement, though that other party may itself be a coalition of nations. It is up to each party to determine if the agreement is being kept, not any outside multinational or supra-national body. The national government should only have the authority to enter into bilateral trade agreements.

What they are empowered to agree to is another matter. Certainly they should be in charge of inspecting goods entering into the nation for safety. They should have the power to ban the importation of items they feel are unsafe. They should be permitted to impose duties or tariffs on such goods to some degree.

Tariffs are a tax on those who consume goods from outside the nation. No one likes taxes, but some tax is necessary to fund the legitimate operations of government. Better a tax on imported goods than one on individual incomes. It's more the national government's business as to what enters our borders than it is their business to know the income of an individual citizen.

Everything said above as it relates to trade agreements should be applied to other areas as well. For example, multi-party treaties on the environment surrender national sovereignty just as much as, or even more than, multi-party trade agreements.

I would suggest a two-tiered authority for tariffs from the central government. Only a low level would be allowed, perhaps only up to a tenth-part of the value of the good, on products from nations who have freedom of currency such as a localist nation would, or whose currency is redeemable for a metal having the seven properties of money. For nations which do not have sound money or freedom of money, there should be no restrictions on the ability of the national government to tariff, nor should the co-sovereigns be so restricted. Let there be a multi-layered wall of protection between the people and economies which mandate the use of fiat money.

The reason for this relates to something we have mentioned before: The ability of those who run a fiat currency to print it out of thin air and buy up the world with it before the world realizes that the value in that paper has been diluted away. A direct way for such a crime to occur would be for them to print it over there, bring it over here, and directly trade it for all of your real estate and money-backed metal. Another less direct way they could implement such a scheme is to run their own economy with such paper, and then trade the goods they manufactured using fiat money for your real money. It's the same scam with an intermediate step.

For this reason, it is right and proper for an economy with real money or even better, freedom of money, to wall itself off from one which operates on fiat money.

Fiat money produces distortions that can in the end bring down not only that economy, but any economy vitally connected to it. All sorts of games can be played with paper money that will result in the massive misallocation of resources. When the consequences for that misallocation finally come home, it will be ugly.

Free trade is a good thing, but it is a perilous quest when one of the partners operates under a fiat money monopoly. Holding a large amount of another country's fiat currency requires a degree of trust among foreign nations that rarely is to be found in this world even between two friends.

If I trade with a man and give him gold for his goods, or he for mine, then we both can be sure that what we got in the exchange will still be the same a year from now. This is not true of fiat paper. Those who control fiat paper can take the goods in exchange for paper, and then create more currency which sucks the value from the money that was just given to the "trading partner." Conversely, a nation might greatly reduce the value of its currency ahead of the trade in order to artificially boost their exports. Too many games can be played in either direction.

Tariffs are taxes, and it is a desirable thing to have tariffs as low as possible as much as it is to have all other taxes low. But given that taxes have to be levied, it is better that the central government exist on tariffs than off of almost any other type of tax. Since their primary duties are to deal with other nations, it is only fitting that their support comes from foreign trade. It is foreign banks and foreign interests which have benefitted from shifting the burden of paying for our federal government from tariffs to taxes on income.

Let local governments, if need be, rely on taxes of income or property, or taxes on the sale of goods. All such taxes make it the government's business to know the business of the citizen, what property they own, from where they derive their living, and how they might spend what they have earned. Such information is power, and such power ought to be dispersed among the various co-sovereigns and localities rather than accumulated all in one place.

A Third Lesson: On the Power to Regulate Interstate Commerce

Now as to the power to regulate trade among the states, if it is impossible for the nation to enter a multi-party trade agreement without sacrificing some of its sovereignty, then it must also be impossible to put the central government in charge of regulating interstate commerce without the co-sovereigns giving up some of their sovereignty. Let us then be careful as to how much power to "regulate interstate commerce" is given to the central government.

The power to regulate trade amongst the co-sovereigns has been vastly expanded and egregiously abused by our current federal government. There was even a case (*Wickard*) where crops a farmer grew on his own land to feed his own livestock was judged to be subject to federal regulations on those crops under the "interstate commerce clause." The excuse used by the judges was that if he had not used his crops to feed that livestock, then he might have had to buy them on the market, and therefore his private use of grain on his own land could have "affected" interstate commerce!

This is a usurpation of authority by the federal government. The Constitution only authorizes them to regulate commerce *between* the states, not commerce *within* states which might have some effect on commerce between the states.

The power to regulate interstate commerce must be limited to goods or services directly flowing from one state to another, and not reaching to any previous or following added value imparted to those goods or services as a result of economic activity which occurs within the borders of a single co-sovereign.

In addition, in a localist nation two states may, with regard to economic activity among themselves, agree to suspend any law from the central government whose authority is based on the power to regulate interstate commerce, save that the governments of adjacent states have the authority to file suit to federal court to overturn the suspension if significant loss or harm to them or their citizens can be shown as a direct result of the suspension. As explained before, the judges in such a suit would be drawn from other states.

As an aside, it must be noted that regulatory agencies have been shown to be a terrible way to obtain justice. Those with the strongest motive to influence and take over a regulatory agency are the big players in the industry to be regulated.

This unfortunate tendency results in regulatory agencies which serve the desires of those big players in the industry they are supposed to be "regulating" rather than insure equity in the law. Monsanto might push for regulations which are burdens to small farmers but no burden to itself. These burdensome regulations might be put in place under the guise of "food safety" but the real goal would be to erect barriers to competition.

Suits at common law should be used to reduce pollution and ensure food safety and the like. This is preferable to the establishment of vast and unaccountable regulatory agencies which are attractive targets for capture by trans-national entities.

Regulatory agencies ought to be used, if they must be used, rarely and only with measures in place to protect against capture and corruption. Any federal agency regulating interstate commerce ought to be eligible to be sued on the charge that the agency has been captured by persons or corporations within the industry it is tasked with regulating. The legal remedy for a regulatory agency which has been found *captus quod infectus* should include the replacement of its high officers.

The Fourth Pillar's Central Lesson: On Currency, Money, Credit, and Banking

"The system of banking [is] a blot left in all our Constitutions, which, if not covered, will end in their destruction..." Thomas Jefferson, statement made on revoking the charter of the 1st Bank of the United States in 1811.

"A great industrial nation is controlled by its system of credit. Our system of credit is concentrated. The growth of the Nation and all our activities are in the hands of a few men. We have come to be one of the worst ruled, one of the most completely controlled and dominated Governments in the world - no longer a Government of free opinion no longer a Government by conviction and vote of the majority, but a Government by the opinion and duress of small groups of dominant men." Woodrow Wilson in *The New Freedom* 1913.

"The Federal Reserve Bank of New York is eager to enter into close relationship with the Bank for International Settlements....The conclusion is impossible to escape that the State and Treasury Departments are willing to pool the banking system of Europe and America, setting up a world financial power independent of and above the Government of the United States....The United States under present conditions will be transformed from the most active of manufacturing nations into a consuming and importing nation with a balance of trade against it."- Rep. Louis McFadden - Chairman of the House Committee on Banking and Currency quoted in the *New York Times* (June 1930)

"It is well enough that people of the nation do not understand our banking and monetary system, for if they did, I believe there would be a revolution before tomorrow morning."- attributed to Henry Ford by Russell Maguire in American Mercury (October 1957), p. 79

~~~~~~~~~~~~~~~~~~~~~~~~~~~~~

I have said before that these lessons that we have learned from history form the fourth and central pillar of the seven pillars of Localism. This fourth pillar also has seven lessons, just as localism has seven pillars. Three of these lessons we have discussed already, judicial reform, treaties concerning trade among the nations (which also applies to environmental treaties), and the regulation of interstate commerce.

We come therefore to the fourth lesson of the seven lessons which make up the fourth pillar of the seven pillars. As the fourth pillar is central to the whole edifice, so the fourth lesson is central to the fourth pillar. More space will be devoted to this topic than the other lessons because it is here that the agents of statism find the credit which supplies fuel for all of their other schemes.

The people of a nation are not free so long as an oligarchy has control over their money. One half of every financial transaction we make consists of the currency used to make the purchase. Proverbs reminds us that the borrower is servant to the lender. What better way to subjugate a nation than to devise a financial system that over time inevitably leads them to debt?

The American Middle Class finds itself working harder, but is being methodically stripped of its wealth by a financial system which was designed for that very purpose. Since the American Middle Class has values and beliefs that are anathema to global government, global governance cannot be completed until the American middle class has been robbed of the economic means to resist its ascension.

The Federal Reserve System acts like a magic money machine with the power to create new dollars out of thin air. Those dollars are given value by sucking a bit of the value out of all other existing dollars, including the ones in your paycheck and your bank account. Any group of men who had control over a magic money machine like that would, in time, grow all powerful financially and politically. The villains who control the Federal Reserve System have control of such a machine, and they are, over time, becoming all powerful politically and financially.

The machine must be destroyed. Do everything else in the volume of this work to reform government, but fail to do this, and the rest is for naught. They will simply buy their way back into power with money which they create from thin air. They will enslave the population with fiat dollars whose value comes only from the labors of that very same population. In debt based fiat currency, the citizens are the collateral.

As an activist, monetary policy and banking might not be the aspect of fighting centralized government which interests you, but I tell you that you will never stop globalism without correcting the abuses in money and banking. It is the fountainhead, the ultimate funding source, for all their other schemes.

The key tenet of localism is the decentralization of political power. And make no mistake about it, monetary power is political power. Some rules such as those I propose below are essential to the maintenance of a free society. I define a free society as one in which individuals have real choice and real input into what laws govern them. This cannot be done in a large central state. Decentralization in government is therefore a prerequisite for a free society. Therefore you cannot have both central banking and a decentralized government. You must choose one or the other.

So then, what sort of rules or framework would promote the de-centralization of power in money, currency, and banking? First of all understand that the Constitution was entirely silent on the subject of banking. Those who I would describe as Localists, such as Jefferson, seemed to feel that was a problem. Nevertheless he argued that since the Constitution did not expressly delegate power to the Federal government to charter banks that the federal government had no such power. Alexander Hamilton argued that it was an implied power.

Hamilton won the day and the first central bank of the United States was chartered. It did not have a fraction of the power of our federal reserve today. Would it have gained such over time? It never had the chance, because when Jefferson became President he pulled out all government funds and effectively ended its existence as a central bank. That was the end of the First American War against Central Banking.

Though it is not taught much in government school textbooks, **much of the history of the United**

States consists of a struggle against central banking. Three times bankers have imposed central banks on the nation. The first two attempts were undone by the patriot presidents Thomas Jefferson and Andrew Jackson. Just before Christmas in 1913 the bankers struck again when they slipped the Federal Reserve Act through Congress while few paid attention.

Since that time, the dollar has lost over 95% of its purchasing power. That was after decades of holding a steady value. Where did all that purchasing power from your dollars go over the last 100 years? It was siphoned out of the dollars which you earned and put into new dollars created out of thin air by the bankers. Through circuitous means, they gave those dollars to their friends and to the government.

Imagine dollars as "shares" in a company called "The United States". If there are one million shares and you have one hundred of them, then you own one ten-thousandth of the company. But now imagine the board who controls the company issues another million shares to spend among themselves. Your shares just lost half of their value. That value went to whoever the board gave the newly created shares to.

When real companies do a "stock split" they normally have to double the number of shares which small stock holders like you hold too, not just double the number of shares held by the company itself. But in the case of a central bank, they can double the number of "shares" and give those "shares" to their friends and to the government itself as sort of a bribe to keep the scam going. Politicians love it, because it gives them more money to buy votes with, but most citizens don't realize it for what it is; a hidden tax. Inflation, the dilution of the value of money through additional issuance of currency, is a tax.

Of course the value of the assets in the United States has greatly increased since the inception of the Federal Reserve in 1913. The wealth creation potential of this nation has increased exponentially since that time with technological advances and population growth. That makes it even more astounding that the dollar has lost over 95% of its value.

If a company's share price collapses to 5% of its former value at a time when the value of the assets of the company are soaring, it is a strong indication that the board of directors is issuing shares at an astonishing rate. Unfortunately, too many of these new shares find their way first into the hands of the friends and associates of the people issuing the "shares." This siphons wealth from the other "shareholders" of the country- ordinary Americans.

The other way banks create credit, which is not quite the same as currency but acts like it during booms, is through fractional reserve banking. Banks keep on hand only a small fraction of their total deposits in currency. The rest is loaned or otherwise invested in order to generate revenue.

If a bank has $100 in deposit liabilities but only $4 on hand (with the rest in loans or investments) then it is "leveraged" 25-1. Should some loans go bad, or some investments lose money, and the value of bank assets drop over $4, the bank becomes insolvent.

This is different from a liquidity problem. In a liquidity problem the value of the assets is worth at least 100% of all deposit liabilities, but more depositors want their money back all at once than the bank has on hand. The bank has it tied up in loans and investments. In cases like this the banks normally get the depositor's money by taking loans from other banks, using their good assets as collateral against the loans.

The idea of a Central Bank was sold to Congress with the idea that they could be a "lender of last resort" to banks who needed loans against good collateral to cover temporary "runs" on the bank. What has happened, and what must happen with a government central bank run by bankers themselves, is that favored banks are getting good loans on trash collateral. The loan amount does not reflect the reality that the collateral is trash.

Of late, the system has even forgone the mask of "loans" and has bought trash "assets" from connected banks outright, shifting them to the taxpayer's books. This allows banks to go on operating regardless of their poor investments.

This system serves the role of "moral hazard", that is, something which encourages bad behavior by consistently rescuing actors from the bad consequences of their bad actions, or even rewarding bad behavior.

Imagine someone at the casino. Every winning bet they make, they can keep the profits. Every losing bet they can take it to the Fed Discount Window and sell it or exchange it for a loan whose amount is based on the false premise that this losing bet is worth about as much as it was before we realized it was a losing bet. That's what's going on in our current banking system with the big banks, and it is not the first time it has been tried. Here is what President Andrew Jackson said just before he won the Second American War against Central Banking....

"Gentlemen, I have had men watching you for a long time and I am convinced that you have used the funds of the bank to speculate in the breadstuffs of the country. When you won, you divided the profits amongst you, and when you lost, you charged it to the bank. You tell me that if I take the deposits from the bank and annul its charter, I shall ruin ten thousand families. That may be true, gentlemen, but that is your sin! Should I let you go on, you will ruin fifty thousand families, and that would be my sin! You are a den of vipers and thieves."

{Quote from the original minutes of the Philadelphia committee of citizens sent to meet with President Jackson (February 1834), according to *Andrew Jackson and the Bank of the United States* (1928) by Stan V. Henkels}

We live in a different generation, but it's the same scam. Such a system only encourages wild gambling. The more bets they make, and the riskier, the larger their payoff. How does it end? Eventually, they and their friends will own the world. Once the government bank that took all their losing bets goes under, they will be able to buy out the cash-starved citizens for pennies on the dollar. At that point America will be divided into two classes, those connected to the central bank, and debt slaves.

An important point here is that this economic system is not capitalism. In capitalism, capital is put at risk in hopes of obtaining a reward. Here, there is the illusion that risk can be eliminated through hedging all bets, and thanks to hedging and wild leveraging, there is very little capital either.

The big banks create exotic financial instruments like Credit Default Swaps backed by nothing but leverage, pretend they have value as they sell them to one another. Then when an event occurs which would make these instruments liabilities, they offload the risk to the taxpayers. Without the assumption of risk, and with far more credit and leverage than capital, it's not capitalism.

It's not even really fractional reserve banking, because it's not reserves that back the system. There practically are no reserves. If there were reserves backing the system, banks could pay off their losses from out of those reserves, rather than off-load those losses to the central bank as described by Jackson. Its leverage and off-loading of losses onto the backs of taxpayers that's backing this terminally corrupt global financial system.

This brief narrative describes the problem, but what sort of government structure might guard against these kinds of abuses? The original constitution was sold by the Federalists as a document which would preserve local autonomy. So as with the judiciary, let's take a look at the provisions in that document which were established as a bulwark against the accumulation of power via the issuance of currency. And since those safeguards have proven inadequate to accomplish the purpose for which they were intended, we can then progress to the subject of how we might strengthen them.

As Jefferson complained, the Constitution was silent with regard to whether or not the Federal government could charter a national bank. Hamilton argued that it was an implied power related to the coining and regulation of money. Jefferson disagreed since an implied power had to be both "necessary and proper" to the exercise a granted power. That proved to be too vague a restriction of implied powers. It is the view of Hamilton which currently prevails.

There was another question which the constitution left open, and that was whether Congress could issue currency not backed by gold or silver, or whether it could issue currency but only that redeemable in gold or silver coin, or whether they had only the power to coin money, leaving to private banks the issuance of any bills of credit or "notes."

Originally notes, such as the currency you now hold, were issued by various banks, and the notes for various banks looked different. Indeed they were different. A note issued by a bank was backed by that bank, and so some bank notes were of dubious value. This sort of dollar bill (or note) was a promise by that bank to pay a specific amount in United States coin when redeemed at the bank. If the bank was trustworthy its bills were used as if they were the coins themselves.

There is a lot I am leaving out here. Early in our history dollar notes from various state banks were the only dollar "bills" around. Later there were periods, before Congress taxed them out of existence, that dollar "bills" or notes issued by state banks freely circulated and competed with dollar notes or "bills" issued by the federal Treasury and circulated by nationally chartered banks. Throughout almost all of this time, paper money was created as a debt instrument redeemable for a stated amount of gold or silver coin.

Currency redeemable in gold or silver coin was a way for even the common man to exercise a mini-veto over the fiscal policies of his government. As long as a man felt that the government (with associated banks) was not overspending or over-leveraging by printing too much paper currency relative to their actual reserves of real money, he could accept the currency in a transaction as if it were "as good as gold" (or silver). But if he began to suspect that the government was over-issuing currency he could take that currency to a bank and have it exchanged for specie.

If enough citizens did that, the government was effectively blocked from spending more money through the issuance of additional currency. They were limited to issuing currency in quantities proportional to the amount they could back with specie.

Since this system presented citizens with what amounted to a personal veto on profligate government spending, those who ran the government enacted various schemes by which they relieved themselves of their obligations to fully redeem currency. The problem with government currency backed by specie is that the government seeks every opportunity to alter the rules so as to shake free of their obligation to the citizen to back it faithfully.

Another issue is that of "legal tender." While Congress was given the power to coin money and regulate its value, it was not given explicit power to make the use of either its coin or any currency backed (or un-backed) by its coin a "legal tender." That is, it was not given the explicit power to mandate the acceptance of its coins or notes for payment of debt.

Freedom from legal tender laws gives individuals the power to refuse to use money when they feel its quality is suspect. Conversely, legal tender laws serve the interests of those who peddle unsound money. They force people to use a type of money as a store of value, even when they suspect that said money is leaking value due to the mismanagement or even dishonesty of those who control its issue.

States are forbidden to coin their own money by the Constitution. That power was reserved to the Federal government. On the other hand the states were granted power to make something a legal tender, but only if was of gold or of silver. In other words, they could not make paper claims on gold or silver legal tender, but only actual gold or silver.

Localism would go beyond even these constitutional measures in that it would take the power to issue money away from the government altogether. The closest they could get is that local government could issue, on a vote of the people, discrete amounts of scrip, so long as such issue was regulated by the state and backed by payment in real money (more on that in a bit). Scrip so denominated is properly a credit instrument, not money.

The issuer of the money holds the money up as being a secure store of value. But what happens when government, as an issuer of money, violates this implied contract? Government cannot be an honest enforcer of a contract to which they are a party. But I get ahead of myself. Let us turn now to possible solutions in the realm of money and banking.

Solutions on Money, Currency, and Banking

~~~~~~~~~~~~~~~~~~~~~~~~~~

The power to issue currency and define money is so great that it cannot be entrusted to any one set of hands. No one should have a monopoly on money, most especially not the government itself. The government's job is to make sure contracts are enforced. If they are one of the parties to the contract then they have a conflict of interest in enforcing it. Localists advocate removing from government the power to create money.

In the case of money and currency, there is an implied contract that the currency that an issuing entity offers is sound. The government should be the referee to insure that what is used as money is honest. They can't be an honest referee if they grant themselves a monopoly to be one of the parties to that contract. History shows us that governments have repeatedly reneged on the implied contract of the value of their currency. A central government which can make its own money will soon be able to buy up the country it allegedly serves.

Here then, are seven money and banking principles necessary to sustain local self-government. Most of them place the government in the position of neutral enforcer of contracts rather than self-granted monopolists with the power to mandate by law that you use their product. These principles should also prevent a parasitical financial sector from swelling large enough to dominate a nation's government and engulfing the productive economy.

The Seven Principles of Safe Money and Banking

1. The central government should be explicitly barred from chartering banks.

2. No level of government should have the power to coin money, or declare anything a legal tender, save that they can specify what form of payment they wish to receive on debts owed directly to them, save that any payments from a co-sovereign to the central government may be in

gold, or in silver, or in a currency or note which the co-sovereign itself accepts as payment of taxes from its' own citizens.

3. No level of government should have the power to ban or tax exchanges or the use of money and money backed currency, counting as money certain metals which possess the seven characteristics of money, which include gold, silver, copper, nickel, platinum, palladium and others. This is not meant to be a ban on sales taxes, but rather a ban on taxes against the use of specific types of real money.

4. Each co-sovereign agrees to insure that each deposit bank, which shall be separate from investment banks, chartered within its borders has a reserve of money (the asset, normally metal, not a paper claim on the asset) on which they can lay their hands within one day equal to at least 20 percent of the value of all bank deposits. Further, that the net value of the assets minus liabilities on a bank's books plus their reserve capital is sufficient to settle all issuances of paper liabilities (such as a bank currency), and cover deposits. In the case of a default or failure to settle the Officers and

Directors of Banks are *personally liable* for the assets of the bank. The bank inspectors and regulators of the co-sovereign shall be bonded against the failure of a bank under their purview.

5. The use of interest must be greatly curtailed and loan activity converted to a partnership or planned re-purchase agreement basis.

6. Currencies backed by something other than money metals are permitted, but their use may be taxed. The central government generally and the co-sovereigns individually within their territories, retain the right to tax, tariff, and restrict or ban the use of, foreign or domestic currency which is not redeemable in a metal possessing the characteristics of money.

7. Neither governments nor banks are permitted to do their own minting, nor are minters permitted to issue notes or currency against their own inventory. Minting of money is privatized and is separated from the creation of currency, which is also private. "Coins" are simply private brands of minted rounds which are approved by some co-sovereign for payment of taxes or direct transactions with that co-sovereign. The more

Localism, a Philosophy of Government

brands the co-sovereign will accept, the better it is for the people.

"Redeemable in metal" in each case above means redeemable for a pre-defined amount of money-metal, not merely that one could use the currency or note to purchase a varying quantity of metal.

I believe that these seven restrictions represent the fewest number consistent with maintaining the decentralization of power necessary to preserve the liberty of the citizens. Money and the ability to create credit are extremely powerful. If there are not rules set out beforehand to diffuse these powers, then those who come to wield them will afterward set up rules so that they will be increasingly concentrated.

The first rule needs no explanation, and the second little explanation. It has already been explained that the power to coin money is too great to be entrusted to the government. But government should also be limited in power to define what is used for money, lest they prop us some un-backed paper with artificial value by declaring it the only form of "money" it will take in payment of taxes.

~ 101 ~

Since the central government is forbidden to lay a direct tax on individual citizens of the co-sovereigns (more on that in a bit), most demands for tax payments will come in the form of taxes on corporations doing business in more than one state, tariffs, or money from a co-sovereign as its "share" of some federal program.

Even in that last scenario, the central government alone should not dictate what form of money is used for payment of any taxes which might be due it. Any form of money good enough for the co-sovereign to accept as payment for its own taxes ought to be good enough for the central government to accept as payment for theirs.

Item three also needs little explanation. The federal government has in the past levied taxes on transactions made in any currency propagated by a state bank in an effort to force people into using its own currency. The power to tax is the power to destroy. That phrase was used in a court decision which ruled that state governments have no power to tax federal banks. The courts did not rule the other way though- they permitted the federal government to destroy the use of bank notes from state chartered banks by placing additional taxes on their use. This 3rd principle is designed to ban taxation on any sound money from any source, counting even the metals with the properties of money as money.

Item four may need more explanation. There is a lot of confusion about "fractional reserve banking." Archimedes once said "Give me a lever long enough and I shall move the world." Leverage is a powerful force, and it's true that localism is all for the decentralization of power. But on close inspection the financial disasters we have seen recently were not caused by fractional reserve banking, because to have fractional reserve banking one must have reserves. Reserves were not backing this system, because there were practically no reserves available. The big banks were all leveraging 20, 30 or even 100 to one against their assets.

Leveraging one's assets 100 to 1 certainly allows for great powers of asset accumulation during boom periods. During contractions or miscalculations though, the great power unleashed is one of financial destruction. The big banks thought they could replace an adequate reserve ratio with financial instruments that acted as hedges. Or perhaps I should say pseudo-hedges, since no one seems to have accumulated reserves of capital as a buffer against a chain-reaction of failures to perform.

The power to create credit through fractional reserve banking must be limited. Some prefer that it be abolished altogether, and believe that it is intrinsically unethical. I find these conclusions place an unnecessary degree of restriction on voluntary economic activity, for reasons that are beyond the scope of this work. I would compare it to fire, a dangerous servant, but a useful one that ought to be contained but not banned. The thing is to devise rules which keep that fire from burning our economy down.

Were there no requirements for banks to hold back reserves, in boom times the most money will be made by those who use the most leverage. That makes the boom even bigger, and encourages even more players to sacrifice reserves. At that point any shock to the system will initiate a cascade of failures ending in catastrophe. That is why it is in everyone's interest to make sure all banks are playing by the same rules as regards to how much leverage they can use.

The difficulty is that politicians have every incentive to keep credit loose and keep the economy artificially pumped up. If we place them in charge of making sure banks have a reserve requirement we must also fix it so that the politicians don't profit at the ballot box when banks are allowed to cheat and flood the system with easy money.

The foxes have a disincentive to insure that the hen house is well guarded. Here, we give both those running the banks and the government incentive to really make sure banks are in order by making its regulatory officers, and officers of the bank, personally responsible for depositor losses. Again this would be in real money that they cannot just create out of thin air should a bank operator become insolvent.

This policy completely reverses the incentive to steal which is built into the current system. The current system has "regulators" with no incentive to regulate. Indeed there is a revolving door between the regulators and the banks they are supposed to watch. Operators have little incentive not to loot, since they can leave and the government simply replaces the funds at taxpayers' expense to maintain "the health of the system." We eliminate the current incentive of bank operators and state regulators to loot the banks by making them personally liable if the bank becomes insolvent.

States will probably have the banks pay an insurance fee, much like a state-level FDIC (or preferably a privatized version thereof), as an emergency fund to use in case a bank fails. The current FDIC is a sham. The fees charged to the banks can't begin to cover potential losses at these levels of leveraging. The system knows it can just print funny money to cover the difference anyway.

As to the fifth principle, students of the Judeo-Christian tradition will observe that in the Old Testament the use of interest was extremely restricted. One Israelite could not make a loan at interest to another. They could only loan at interest to a foreigner. Loans to one another were probably made on the basis of a split ownership with a pre-arranged agreement for the borrower to buy the loaner out, or simply remain in partnership.

Of course it is not necessary to believe in the veracity of scripture to accept the benefits of restricting the use of interest by law. You need not hold that the scripture is always right, merely that it is not always wrong. The rational mind will not reject a good idea simply because of personal prejudice against its source. For the reader who prides themselves on their pragmatism I ask, is the financial house constructed by post-modern banking really more stable and beneficial to mankind now that humanity has rejected scriptural principles on finance as a cornerstone?

When we look at our domestic economy today we see how the crushing burden of compounding interest comes to overwhelm an economy. We see people making mortgage payments for the cream of their adult lives, yet still not owning their own homes. The financial sector swells in size even as the manufacturing sector contracts. Our best minds are now devoted to trading paper back and forth among themselves while our infrastructure crumbles and local businesses are starved for credit.

In short, we see myriads of problems that would not exist if the use of interest in domestic loans were banned and the borrower had some say in the assignability of the loan (as would be the case if loans were legally viewed as a partnership). Banks would not extend credit to anyone with a heartbeat on the grounds that they could just sell or securitize the loan. They would not loan money on trash assets. They would once again be incentivized to provide due diligence because they would be looking for investment partners, not just rubes.

Under such a system banks would have an incentive to work for the success of the borrower/partner, rather than an incentive to pump up their debt via easy credit in good times, only to yank credit back at a key moment. A coordinated withdrawal of credit by a few giant banks would precipitate widespread default, allowing them and their controllers to grab the assets of a nation at a bargain price during an induced collapse in economic activity. Society should have a firewall in place against such an eventuality, and the one we propose would smooth out the booms and busts of what is called the "business cycle."

Interest rates are a tool by which the flow rate of money to an economy can be varied. And whoever has their hand on the throttle which controls that flow rate has great power. A whole nation, and its government, can all too easily find themselves on the wrong end of the power of compound interest. It is no wonder that the Mosaic Law banned interest in order to prevent the people from winding up as debt slaves, nor is it any wonder that because we have disregarded the principles expounded upon in the Divine Law that something much like debt slavery is upon us.

Regarding point six, there are other things besides metals that could back a currency. Fiat currency is backed by a promise to extract wealth yet to be produced from a given population. Oil or gasoline might back a currency. These items don't really possess the seven characteristics of money though. And since there is a large supply of "other things" out there, the potential for flooding the economy with alternative but inferior money exists.

Suppose gasoline, toilet paper, toothpaste and a hundred other things all get "monetized", that is, become the backing for a private currency? This can lead to the same sort of credit boom, and following painful bust, that we have suffered through. There must be a mechanism to limit the growth of pseudo-money while still decentralizing the power of being able to define money. The balanced position is to permit the government to tax the use of money backed by things which don't possess the seven characteristics of honest money, as the money metals do, but deny them the power to tax the use of honest money.

The problem of fiat or weak currency infecting an economy is not limited to such currency originating within one's own borders. What prevents a foreign nation with a fiat currency from printing up ten trillion dollar's worth of it and buying out half your country before people figure out the inflation effects of such printing makes their newly acquired currency nearly worthless? They gave you stacks of their depreciating paper for your real assets. Pseudo-capital controls against fiat money flowing in are not an obstacle to free trade so much as a protection against fraud.

Fiat money at home has given "capital controls" a bad name. Such controls have typically been used to force people to use the government's own money even when they believed it unsound. In localism, the government has no money, and therefore the abuse of capital controls in this manner would be impossible. But perhaps we should find a more accurate term to describe these powers in localism: Government is not actually authorized to control capital, but only debt masquerading as capital.

In trying to return to honest money so that we might build a society that is not controlled by bankers, we must not only prevent our own bankers from buying the country with money they print from thin air, but we must also take steps to insure that foreign bankers are blocked from doing so. This extends beyond taxing fiat currencies. When we discuss trade, we will see that nations try a complicated version of the scam I describe above by deliberately weakening their currencies to pump up their exports. That version of the scam must also be addressed, and may be done so by the judicious use of tariffs.

Point seven is a separation of powers issue. The concern is that a cartel of minting banks could enforce significant seigniorage on the coins they mint. While the potential for abuse is far less than that attainable by the "magic money machine" of fiat currency, separating these functions should help keep the premium from seigniorage down to a reasonable level.

"One of the evils of paper money is that it turns the whole country into stock jobbers. The precariousness of its value and the uncertainty of its fate continually operate, night and day, to produce this destructive effect. Having no real value in itself it depends for support upon accident, caprice, and party; and as it is the interest of some to depreciate and of others to raise its value, there is a continual invention going on that destroys the morals of the country." – Thomas Paine, from a larger pamphlet on government written in 1786. It appears in the Complete Writings of Thomas Paine, edited by Philip Foner, Citadel Press, 1945, pp. 405ff

A Fifth Lesson: National Debt & Direct Taxes

~~~~~~~~~~~~~~~~~~~~~~~~

Even under a sound system of money and baking, debt as a means of control is still a possibility. It is possible to have a sound system of money and banking, but still have an unsound level of public and/or private debt. There were debt slaves even in the ancient world, when coinage was sound and banking systems simpler. Measures to guard against excess debt may therefore be contemplated separately from the issues of money and banking.

Alexander Hamilton was in favor of national debt as a sort of "glue" to bind the states together. At that time, it was assumed that states could leave the union if they wished, and he wanted national debt as a way to make any separation a messy matter. For a localist, two groups of people who dislike each other and have irreconcilable ideas about how civil society ought to be conducted should not be forced to remain in political union simply because they owe bankers public money. National debt must be abolished.

Though we make every effort to limit the central government's function, and prohibit the issue of debt-based currency (or any other currency) by the national government, there might still be times when debt is required. Funding national defense in time of war is the prime example. In such a case, the debt instruments issued ought be tied to a specific co-sovereign and issued by them at the request of the central government on an apportioned basis, either by share of the population or share of national income.

This has many advantages over our present course. Instead of making debt easy and separation difficult, it makes debt more difficult and separation, if necessary, easier. Nothing will encourage the national government to be more courteous and respectful of the states than the knowledge that the states can leave if they are mistreated, and that national borrowing can come only through them.

Conversely, nothing will encourage employees of the national government to treat the states with more contempt than the knowledge that the states are under bondage to remain in the union regardless of how poorly they are treated. Add to it this; in our present system the other states would join with the national government in preventing an amicable departure on account of shared national debt.

In our current system state officials serve the interests of the central government rather than the interests of their own citizens. The reason for this is that the states get some of this borrowed federal money, which appears "free" to them. With the scourge of direct taxation, the individual citizen bears the burden of repayment of money that the central government gives to the states.

National government borrows on the account of ordinary citizens through national debt, and then gives some of the money to state governments.

State governments then side with the national government even against the interests and wishes of their own citizens. The central government uses money borrowed against the account of the citizens to induce their own state governments to act against their will.

Making all borrowing, and collecting as well, come through the states completely reverses this dynamic. Each time the state is handed a request from the central government to issue debt for their benefit, the state officials are highly motivated to use their influence to curb the national spending which makes such borrowing necessary.

This lesson of history is called "National Debt." Up to this point I have been more accurately speaking of "Public Debt" or "Government Debt." But a government is not a nation. Rather, nations are made from people and they have governments. A comprehensive view of "National Debt" must include a private debt component.

In the Old Testament, God provided economic rules which were designed to prevent society from stratifying into a few very wealthy over a much larger group of citizens who lived in perpetual grinding poverty. Not that everyone was to be equal. Private property rights were respected to a greater degree than in our current law. There was no maximum amount of wealth that any family could acquire, and coveting the possessions of your neighbor was counted a grievous sin.

Still, the Old Testament did not treat all wealth as being of equal worth to society. The wealth earned through providing goods and services of value to your neighbors was protected in law. What was banned was wealth generated through oppression, using influence with the government to render an unjust decision in one's favor, and enticing one's neighbors into getting on the wrong side of "the miracle of compounding interest." In short, wealth which increased the size of the pie was treated differently than wealth which merely re-divided the pie.

At the same time there were other economic rules which insured that no family had to endure multi-generational poverty. While there was no limit to how rich an individual family could become, so long as they came by it honestly, there were also rules in place which fostered a healthy middle class. There were rules which kept wealth, and thus political power, from becoming so centralized that localities would lose their economic power and political independence.

A vibrant middle class is essential to the dispersion of political power (and thus it is no wonder that the centralizers have enacted policies which deliberately wage war against it). Since it is also our goal to preserve large amounts of autonomy for localities, the principle presented in scripture designed for a similar purpose should be instructive to us today.

We have already discussed the prohibition on interest in loans to real persons who were fellow citizens. This limited the growth on debt and removed the "miracle of compound interest" as a tool of debt enslavement. The other rule ordained to preserve what amounted to a "middle class" was the law of Jubilee.

By that law, each 50th year all debts were cancelled. Lands (at least rural lands) were "super-Allodial" in the sense that they could not be sold. They could only be leased for 49 years. In the 50th year they would return to the heir in the original family.

Jubilee was not unjust as are many plans of "debt forgiveness" floated today, because lenders and borrowers knew the rules well in advance. This was the law of Jubilee. It ensured that one bad family member could not wreck his family's fortunes for generations. A profligate son could only blow it for his own generation. His son or his grandson would not live life in a hole dug by his father or grandfather. Rather, the wishes of the profligate son's own father or grandfather to pass down some of his wealth would be respected. It also meant that it would be impossible for some small group to slowly gather up most of the real wealth in the nation. There would never be a small elite group with all the assets in the nation overseeing a vast horde of landless and indebted serfs.

Obviously for justice to be maintained the lenders and borrowers must have ample notice that a Jubilee is approaching. As it nears, credit is likely to be restricted. That too can be anticipated and provision can be made for it. Far from a liability, this feature is a protection. People can't get in too much trouble as the Jubilee approaches.

Bear in mind that credit always tightens at some point in every market system. The only question is timing and knowledge. Will this tightening occur at a time known to all, or will it be the decision of a few sprung on the nation at a time when people least expect it?

Which is better, a known point in time in which credit will be restricted, or is it better to leave the decision in the hands of a few giant banks as to when credit will be restricted? Is it not better that the rules are known to all than to have individuals and businesses get strung out on "easy credit" only to have a small cartel of credit merchants make a surprise decision to tighten up?

The concept of jubilee is far more just than our current system where individuals can abuse bankruptcy laws, and large lenders can abuse everyone.

With respect to government debt, our present system is madness because it essentially allows the federal government to decide how much money it wants to print and borrow. A localist would only allow central government borrowing to occur through the states, and thus be dependent on them for credit rather than the reverse situation we now face.

Government debts are paid with taxes. When the U.S. Constitution was drafted, the Founders wisely forbade the national government from collecting what it called "direct taxes" from the citizens. What did that mean exactly? Unfortunately the centralizers lawyered their way around this being a ban on the national government taxing the income of citizens. But some people lawyered back. After the *Pollock* case, taxes on income from certain sources was ruled to be a direct tax and thus unconstitutional. As a result they passed the 16th amendment to make legal that which they had previously done.

The result is that the federal government now has the power to intimidate and silence almost any citizen with a decent income. Washington D.C. has a built-in mechanism to track and put its finger on any one of us. The tax code is riddled with special interest loop holes as business learns it is more profitable to lobby congress than please customers. The tax code has become so complex that not even IRS employees know what's legal, yet somehow citizens are responsible for the result.

Under localism the Constitution's ban on direct taxes from the federal government would be not only returned, but strengthened. No individual's income from any source could be taxed by the central government. The federal government would have no grant of authority to compel citizens to report to them their income or from whence it was derived. Under localism, the central government would have no national tax power to hold over any individual citizen.

The national government would be funded by tariffs, taxes on multi-state corporations, fees for specific services, and by states paying their share of the federal government bill on a per capita or "share of GDP" basis. Unless you sought a specific service from the federal government, such as patent registration, state government would always be a shield between you and the central government.

It's really none of the central government's business how much money an individual citizen makes or from what source they derive their income. It may be your state's business, but you can change states a lot more easily than you can change nations. Power closer to home is much easier to call to account than power afar off. If your state makes a mess of their tax code as badly as the feds have mismanaged theirs, you can more easily both fix the problem (by political action) or escape the state, as you prefer. Both forces will manifest as pressure for a wayward state to reform its tax code.

A Sixth Lesson: On the Character of the Military

"Political power flows from the barrel of a gun." – Chairman Mao

"The bane of liberty." – Vice President to James Madison Elbridge Gerry on standing armies.

"Of all the enemies to public liberty war is, perhaps, the most to be dreaded because it comprises and develops the germ of every other. War is the parent of armies; from these proceed debts and taxes ... known instruments for bringing the many under the domination of the few.... No nation could preserve its freedom in the midst of continual warfare." — James Madison, *Political Observations*, 1795

~~~~~~~~~~~~~~~~~~~~~~~~~~

Many of the Founders considered standing armies to be a menace to liberty. They objected that the proposed constitution would permit them, but were assured by proponents that the whole mass of citizens being armed would serve to block any threat to liberty from a standing army. As the difference in sophistication and firepower between weapons held by the citizens and those held by the military grows to vast levels these assurances ring hollow. The 2nd amendment should be a floor, not a ceiling, in protecting the rights of Americans against violations by a potential military police state.

In 1861 states attempted to leave the Union and it took years to subdue them. Today they could be subdued in hours. Mao was a rascal, but his most famous quote would not be famous if there wasn't truth in it. Military power has become centralized in the United States from its inception to the current day, as have all other political and governmental powers. Just as with many other powers, the safeguards that the Constitution set out proved to be inadequate to meet its purpose of preventing over centralization.

Decentralization could be assured if the national government had no power to keep troops, but only the power to borrow them from the states. The national government could still run the Navy and Air Force, though states would have no prohibition on having these units if they desired. In time of peace the Defense Department could have a committee which would assess the total need for ground forces and the proportional size of the units needed from each state to meet these goals. That would represent the minimum size Army units a state would be expected to maintain both active duty and reserve. They could recommend equipment suppliers, but each state would make the final decision on those issues.

During a time of declared war the units of the states would be assigned to field commanders picked from among the general officers of the state armies by the Department of Defense. Administratively, they would still be under the control of the states. They would be loaned to the national government, for as long as the Governor of the state and their legislature felt it proper.

Consider the healthy changes this arrangement would bring compared to our current predicament: Instead of the states prodding for more military spending within their boundaries (using money collected from the other states) they would be agitating for less, since they would be paying the bills. Empire would be difficult to maintain since states would balk at paying the bills that the national government would run up in the process. The national government would be less likely to continue unpopular wars fighting with a borrowed army than it would be with its own.

War, the enemy of liberty, would not continue on the whim of the bomb makers, but only by permission of the states and their people. The system would curb imperial ambition in the national government, while still permitting the fielding of an army when the nation truly needed defending.

Best of all, it would be almost impossible for the central government to turn such a military loose on its own population. Right now our national army is largely being trained and conditioned to administer military police states in nations overseas. That raises the risk that this skill set will be used on our own population. In such a case, what we have done to others will be done to us, and we shall pay for the privilege.

A localist would wish that we build our land forces in a decentralized manner. Any inconvenience arising from such a design will be more than compensated for by the reduced chance of an army so constructed from turning its guns on its own populace, or embarking on liberty-destroying imperial wars.

The Seventh Lesson: Corporate Persons

"Merchants have no country. The mere spot they stand on does not constitute so strong an attachment as that from which they draw their gains." – Thomas Jefferson to Horatio G. Spafford, 1814, The Writings of Thomas Jefferson (Memorial Edition), by Lipscomb and Bergh, Volume 14, Page 119, 1920.

~~~~~~~~~~~~~~~~~~~~~~~~~~~~~~~

Corporations are creations of government. They are not natural persons, but rather property – natural persons can own them. They are legal (read government) entities. The idea that corporations might be afforded "rights" as if they were real persons would be alien to the Founders. They viewed rights as a gift of God, not a grant of the state. The situation in which we find ourselves was for the most part unanticipated.

Most citizens who believe that corporations are "people" and have "rights" don't think so because of logic or reason. They think so because they take their political counsel from media figures who are paid by corporations, either directly or through program sponsorship.

Certainly there is nothing about incorporation which confers any special virtue to men. If men need to be restrained by the law from doing others harm singly, then they must also be so restrained when acting together through a corporate entity.

But why is a corporation formed? A corporation is formed so that individuals can act together, greatly increasing their power, in a way that legally limits the liability for any negative outcomes of their behavior. Both these consequences of incorporation, increased power and reduced accountability for their actions, will tend to make them more prone to corruption and more dangerous than a single individual would be on his or her own. The whole idea of the government artificially limiting the liability for one's joint actions creates a moral hazard.

Some of the loudest voices against restrictions on corporations actually dare to accuse us of being "government interventionists" who "don't believe in human freedom or free markets." Excuse me? The very concept of incorporation is a government invention and intervention. The government is granting a group of people artificial protection from liability for the consequences of their joint actions.

If they win, they keep the profits. If they lose and cause a disaster in the process, their losses can be limited to what they put in. The costs would be shifted to others. That's not a free market concept. Why the insistence that purity to free market principles only begins *after* the government has granted corporations a huge artificial advantage over natural persons? If they accept government intervention to gain an advantage, then they ought not to complain if costs accompany it. If they don't care for the costs, let them forego the benefits and operate as a pure partnership.

If Jefferson doubted the fidelity of merchants to their nation, then how much more should we doubt the fidelity of an artificial legal construct merchant called a "corporation" which has no physical feet at all to stand on any ground? Yet because of their aggregate power, they can afford a lobbyist where the average citizen cannot- and deduct the expenses for said lobbyists from taxes due, unlike the average citizen who must take time off work and use a tank of gas to visit even their state capitol.

Corporations can, by PACS and by giving those in their employ extra compensation which is subtly understood to be given for the purpose of contributing to the campaigns of certain candidates, contribute more money to candidates than can the average citizen. They own the media which defines for the average voter who the "acceptable" candidates might be.

Add to it that the largest corporations in this day are global, not merely national, corporations. If a flesh-and-blood merchant's attachment is to their means of gain more than the spot on which they stand, how much less then is that attachment if they are not flesh but rather an artificial construct found in many spots and many nations? Is it not clear that when corporations whose interests are global control your media and political system then your government will become increasingly global in affection despite the fervent desire of the citizens to retain national sovereignty?

We have learned that when measures are not taken to prevent it, corporate interests can swallow up the interests of individual citizens, localities, and even nations. Where their political influence is unfettered, the nation cannot but be subsumed into a global combine. Let us then consider what must be done to preserve the liberty of individuals, localities, states and nations from the post-constitution threat of global corporations capturing governments.

I have already spoken of measures we ought to take to limit corporate influence in political parties and action committees under the third pillar. That is a useful beginning, but only a beginning. Some other measures:

Corporations should be liable for taxation by the national government based on their overseas earnings as well as their domestic earnings. As it stands now, corporations in the United States don't have to pay taxes on their overseas earnings unless they bring them home. Consequently, they don't bring them home. They keep investing them overseas until the "American" corporation has more assets in foreign lands than it does in our own. At that point, what sort of policies do you suppose they might support, those that favor national interests or those which favor global ones?

You might say that if overseas earnings are taxed, our corporations will not open overseas branches, rather individuals from them will start "sister companies" in the other nations that are separate, with separate interests, even though they might trade with the original company. Good. Let each corporation be tied to the well-being of the nation in which it resides rather than looking upon all the nations of the world as a resource to be mined and then abandoned when no longer profitable.

Instead of one giant company, we might have a dozen smaller ones that market similar products in different parts of the world. And is that so bad?

Smaller companies allow for people to be larger in comparison. Economies of scale have limits. At some point, becoming larger does not enable one to serve the market better, but to "become the market" or become "too big to fail." Once this barrier is reached, increased corporate size is more useful for influencing governments than serving customers.

Note this works both ways. If a foreign company wanted to expand to this country, it could also be taxed based on the earnings in the home country. This would essentially prevent foreign nations from operating a corporation here unless almost all of its assets and profits were located in this nation. This should not impede foreigners from investing in this country if money is to be made. It will only change the procedure which they would use to invest. They would be only buying economic opportunity in this nation, not overseas political power on our shores.

Policies which favor national corporations over global ones also helps reserve our military for its legitimate function of defending this nation. Medal of honor winner General Smedley Butler noted in his book "War is a Racket", that once venture capitalists realized they could make more on their money overseas than at home, the money went overseas and our military followed to protect their overseas property.

This is the sort of abuse of our military that ought to end. If a corporation chooses to operate in another nation, it is the responsibility of the government in that other nation to protect its property there. If they fail to do so, then perhaps that corporation should have considered investing domestically for a lower but safer return.

While we are on it, a corporation should only be owned by actual human beings. No corporation should be permitted to own stock in another corporation. This ensures that the "sister companies" are really sisters, and not subsidiaries.

It also closes many loopholes by which management is able to deceive stockholders as to the actual state of the company, or even loot the company. No longer could they shift bad assets to a subsidiary company which then files for a spectacular bankruptcy- after the execs who arranged the fiasco have pocketed giant bonuses based on a false financial picture. No longer could they siphon off the few profitable assets to a subsidiary in which they hold a disproportionate number of shares. Nor could they leverage political power by owning a percentage of a strategic daisy chain of companies.

Corporations were designed to encourage venture capitalism by allowing individuals to risk some of their wealth but limit their liabilities. That is a positive goal which encourages legitimate investment. But allowing companies to spin off subsidiaries also allows them to concentrate the risk of some great liability while protecting the assets of the parent company.

In other words, it protects the assets of corporations from liability, not the assets of people. And by "liability" I mean mostly risk from paying the costs of doing harm to actual persons. So by allowing corporations to own other corporations, we insulate the parent company from the harm it might do to persons! Such an arrangement protects the interests of artificial persons over those of actual human beings.

Imagine DOW chemical starting a tiny subsidiary whose purpose was to conduct certain high-liability, high-risk operations for DOW. Imagine it was caught dumping toxins in a river which resulted in lifelong birth defects in millions of people. DOW wound up with all its profits because it transferred risk to a company created only to shift those risks onto the population if a disaster occurred. Once caught, the subsidiary could simply declare bankruptcy. Its few assets, when sold off, would pay those it hurt a few pennies on every dollar of damages it caused.

That subsidiary would never have been formed on the free market basis of risks and profits. It only existed to house the riskier aspects of its parent company's operations. This is an abuse of incorporation. If the subsidiary company is based on an idea where the risks and profits make sense, then people can be persuaded to form such companies on their own. Corporations should be owned by real humans, not other corporations.

Instead of this simple rule, entire regulatory agencies have grown up around managing the risks of giant conglomerates in their industries. Unfortunately, this makes the agencies ripe targets for regulatory capture by the largest companies. Then those agencies are turned from their purpose and simply become mechanisms by which the largest companies raise barriers to entry in order to restrict competition.

The issue of corporate lobbyists ought to be addressed as well. Instead of being tax deductible, corporate expenses related to lobbying ought to be fully taxed, and perhaps even double taxed. Somehow, we need to get our businesses back to marketing to consumers to purchase products of their own free will instead of lobbying the government to force citizens to purchase a corporation's products against the consumer's will.

****

The final three pillars of localism..

The Fifth Pillar: On Public Education

"The more subsidized it is, the less free it is. What is known as "free education" is the least free of all, for it is a state-owned institution; it is socialized education - just like socialized medicine or the socialized post office - and cannot possibly be separated from political control." – Frank Chodorov

"Wherever is found what is called a paternal government, there is found state education. It has been discovered that the best way to insure implicit obedience is to commence tyranny in the nursery." – Benjamin Disraeli

"In the hands of the state, compulsory public education becomes a tool for political control and manipulation -- a prime instrument for the thought police of the society. And precisely because every child passes through the same indoctrination process -- learning the same "official history," the same "civic virtues," the same lessons of obedience and loyalty to

the state -- it becomes extremely difficult for the independent soul to free himself from the straightjacket of the ideology and values the political authorities wish to imprint upon the population under its jurisdiction." – Richard Ebeling

"If the only motive was to help people who could not afford education, advocates of government involvement would have simply proposed tuition subsidies." – Milton Friedman

"In all countries, in all centuries, the primary reason for government to set up schools is to undermine the politically weak by convincing their children that the leaders are good and their policies are wise." - Marshall Fritz

"Government schooling is the most radical adventure in history. It kills the family by monopolizing the best times of childhood and by teaching disrespect for home and parents...." – John Taylor Gatto

"[A]ny provider that commands 90 percent of the market—whether we're talking about software, phone service, or heating oil—is, by definition, a monopoly. Our government employs thousands of bureaucrats to *track down and break up monopolies on the grounds that monopolies stifle competition and thereby produce bad products at high prices. Doesn't it strike anyone as strange that the same government protects its own monopoly in education?"* – Jennifer Grossman

"Government will not fail to employ education to strengthen its hands and perpetuate its institutions." – William Godwin

****

A localist understands the folly of ceding to the national government effective control of public education. Even centralized control at the state level is too central. In the localist view, education is the responsibility of the family, and any community schools should be an extension of the family. Any schooling in which the state assists the parents should be built upon this idea, and any schooling which the parent does without assistance from the state should be protected by this idea.

In a nationalized school system, there are conflicts over what values should or should not be taught as various groups contend for the prize of imposing their moral agenda on the next generation. Schools teach morality (and religion, even if it is state or nature worship) to the lowest common denominator in their system. A locally controlled school will have a higher lowest common denominator than a state one, and a state one will be higher than a national one. In a large and diverse country, an education system with national control will be more amoral and educate children more against the wishes of their parents than any other configuration.

So what would the education of children look like in a localist government? Since different places will make different choices, there is no one right answer. Some localities might 1) reject the very notion of "public schooling", even on a community basis, preferring to leave it a purely private endeavor. Others might want it to be 2) as centralized as possible much like we have now. Others, perhaps the largest group, will look 3) for something in between. Under localism, everybody can win. All groups can get their way for their own children in their own community. What localism prohibits is people having their own way with other people's children in other communities.

In describing some measures to help decentralize education we must take into consideration flows of money and disposition of existing assets. For example, and in consideration of options 2 and 3 above, I see no fundamental reason why public school facilities could not house within them two sub schools run by different principles (and perhaps even Principals though not necessarily so).

Parents could choose which type of classes they wanted their children to attend. One would be the community school model, the other the state controlled school model. The same board of education, elected by parents, would be over both sub schools, but the community side would have significantly more freedom to determine curriculum, hiring, and policy than they would with the state-controlled side of things.

This is basically offering parents a choice of whether they want their child's classroom operated on a *en loco parentis* basis where teachers are agents of the parent (as we did prior to the 1970s), or send them to classrooms where the teacher operates as an agent of the state (as is now the case).

Many people fail to appreciate the fundamental change which occurred to education once teachers were legally considered agents of the state rather than agents of the parents. The courts ruled, justifiably for once I think, that teachers could not operate as agents of the parents (with the legal ability to operate in place of the parent) when the parent had no choice other than to accept the teacher's decisions.

That was the original reason given for making teachers agents of the state. It meant that teachers could do less against the parent's wishes, but it also meant they could do less *for* the child in behalf of the parent even in accordance with their wishes. Since that time education expenditures have skyrocketed without a commiserate increase in educational achievement or improvement in moral character.

Teachers could even be split among the two academies. They could teach under the state model for periods 1, 3, and 5, and teach under the community model for the other periods. Such an arrangement takes all the reason for fighting away for those who argue over things like whether or not teachers should be permitted to pray with students or quote religious scripture with students, or discipline a certain way, or what have you.

Some of you might think that some such issues have already been decided by the Supreme Court. And they have in the dusty law books, but what occurs on the ground in the schools of our vast heartland with tacit parental approval is another matter. That's because not everyone agrees with the edicts of our black-robed overlords with respect to the education of our own children- nor in my view should they be compelled to.

Under a dual school model, if a parent does not care for what is going on in these areas with respect to their child in a given class then they can simply move them over to the other sub school, perhaps even just for that class. If I trust Mrs. Johnson then I will ask that my child be placed in her class in a community-model period. In time, the teachers who are trusted by the community will be given more classes where they have more freedom (community model) and those who the parents do not trust will not (state model). Individual empowerment of both parents and teachers cannot fail to produce more satisfactory outcomes than our current top-down system.

Everybody wins, except for the control freaks who simply cannot rest until they have seized control of your child's education from you over and against your wishes. They lose in such a system, but their loss is a glorious gain for families, true education, and the purest goal of government, human liberty.

Some states currently have very large school districts with a number of school facilities. In the localist view, some of those systems ought to be split up, or some method enacted of giving parent groups in that locality more power to direct the community based sub schools in their own community. After all, in 1940 there were 117,000 school districts (in a nation of 132 million people). By 2010 that number had collapsed to only 15,000 districts. We have been concentrating public education for decades now. Maybe it has gone too far.

At the very least, the tendency toward forced consolidation of school districts based on size ought to be stopped. The same goes for "standards" that are a back-door means to close schools down based on small size. Adding "required" courses to be offered is a favorite tactic of those seeking to consolidate their power in education. Is a school which teaches 25 classes well really a worse school than one which teaches 50 classes poorly?

At this point it is necessary to discuss the flow of money and what precautions might be made to balance the desire to ensure children across a state have access to adequate education resources with the desire to preserve local control of schools. If each community completely funded its own school you would again have a situation of rich enclaves attempting to form their own districts and leave poorer areas without adequate resources for even a baseline educational system.

I want to clarify that this point is not made in an effort to ensure all public schools offer "equal" educational opportunities. That would be socialism, not localism. The goal here is to provide opportunity for a statewide floor for education funding, but let each community decide how high its own ceiling is, and who will be under it.

Basic education is a good that benefits not only the recipient, but also society as a whole. Such goods are often consumed at levels that are sub-optimal for society unless they are to some extent subsidized. Parents are often most strapped for cash at the exact time of life they most need outside help in educating their children. If they use the service, taxing them for public education simply takes money from them at a time of life they can most afford it and returns that money to them in services at a time when they need it the most.

What I propose, using a broad definition of school, is that the role of state government in education be limited to 1) suggesting minimum voluntary standards for all schools and mandatory enforceable standards only for those schools which assent to the state controlled model and 2) providing a baseline per pupil funding level which must be the same for all pupils whether designated a school by the state or only by the county, and regardless of whether or not the school assents to state control and 3) authority to designate additional schools not designated by the county to receive such funds. The state would have no other authority to appropriate any other funds for public schools. That's it. Everything else is left to the localities.

Notice that while the state could designate additional parties to which counties must disburse funds, the state cannot deny funds to schools which the county approves but the state does not. Local taxes for education should seldom pass through the state's hands.

In addition, the state's baseline funding should be distributed on a county wide basis. The county will then disburse the money to school districts it feels are qualified, and to any school that the state feels is qualified that the county did not include. The county is authorized to secure baseline funding even for "private" schools or home school associations, if any of them make a strong enough impression on their neighbors to be deemed worthy of public support. It is the counties which decide which institutions get the baseline funding, and the state which determines what the baseline amount per pupil should be, except that the state can choose to fund a school within a county even if the county does not approve.

The counties would be responsible for getting accurate enrollment data which would form the basis for the amount the state is to remit them for distribution to the schools. Under this arrangement, there would be no incentive for the County to disqualify an otherwise good school from receiving baseline funds out of fear of having to spread its state funds thinner. If the county certifies another school, it only increases the total funds to that county.

Local revenues, such as property taxes, committed to education are another matter. The state may have them send in a baseline amount which would be a major component of the state's own baseline funding, but what it does with the rest would be up to the voters of each county, district, and the schools therein.

As an additional safeguard to the sovereignty of parents in a community over the education of their own children, counties ought to have two more powers, one against the legislative branch and another against the judicial.

As regards to the first, local control of education against intrusions of the state legislature, counties ought to have the right to refuse baseline funding from the state and instead with-hold four-fifths of that amount from its remissions of tax revenues to the state for the purpose of funding education in the county as they see fit. In other words, instead of sending it in to have the state hand it back, if the state starts usurping its authority and attaching strings to the money, counties might simply send in less money to the state, and tell them to keep their money and their strings.

To curb judicial usurpation and abuse, counties should be empowered to hold referendums by which they can vote to overturn a judicial decision relating to a school within their boundaries, except for those relating to the disbursing of state baseline funds to schools of any sort, and limited further only by those cases where the state has determined a school is eligible for such funds but the county has not. The premise behind the principle is simple: If the subject is the education of their own children, the will of the parents in a near locality should prevail over the will of judges in a distant one. "Justice" in such matters is defined by the mass of the parents in the community in preference to the opinions of judges afar off.

Though parents might not always make decisions that people from other parts of the state approve, the children do not belong to the state. The state then, except in individual cases of abuse or incapacity, is not authorized to "hold parents accountable" for the educational choices they make for their children. It is ultimately a personal matter, outside the purview of government.

That statement will shock the weakened mind of the post-modern who dares not imagine that anything is outside the scope of the state. On this issue it is their Maker, not their government, to whom parents must answer. To the extent that the parents accept government assistance in the education of their children, it is rather the state which must answer to the parents.

The Sixth Pillar: On the Balance Between the Co-Sovereigns and Localities

"In these two countries, I saw the ills of the State imputed to an infinity of diverse causes, but never to town liberty.....Only peoples who have only a few or no provincial institutions deny their utility; that is, only those who do not know the thing at all, speak ill of it." - Alexis de Tocqueville in chapter five of his book *"Democracy in America"* –

****

Localism does not ensure good government in every locality. No system of government can replace the need for human virtue. Indeed, the belief that humans are corrupt in the use of power is part of what drives the need for decentralization. Local governments do not have unalienable rights, human beings do, and the goal of localism is not to give maximum power to local governments. Rather it is the maximizing of individual liberty and human freedom even while acknowledging the reality of human evil. Localism is not about local governments, but about individuals- because self-government is the ultimate local government.

Co-sovereign governments are empowered to ensure local governments comply with things such as whatever the co-sovereign has by way of a Bill of Rights. They make laws applicable to their territories. Should a local government implode, the co-sovereign should be empowered to step in and restore order and justice.

Local governments are sub-units of a co-sovereign. But even in this relationship, there ought to be limits. Just as it is wrong for the national capitol to make all decisions for the whole nation, each state capitol ought not to make all such decisions for citizens throughout the state without allowance for local desires.

This could take the form of allowing localities to vote to weaken penalties for criminal acts committed within their boundaries. For example an act which might be a low order felony by state law could be treated as a misdemeanor if committed within a jurisdiction which felt penalties for that act were too harsh.

Of course, localities should still be free, as they are now, to make things crimes up to a limit. It would be a freer nation if there were far fewer state laws, and the decision to make a given behavior criminal was instead decided at the county (or even township) level.

Ultimately though, political sub-units, let's say counties, which have little in common with the majority of their state either have a problem or they are the problem. If they have a problem, they ought to have the tools to fix it. If they are the problem then they may find that they need to fix themselves.

Let's consider the case of California. It's a huge and diverse place: Perhaps too diverse to have one set of people in the state capitol making all of the rules for everyone. Suppose that instead of realizing that and permitting the counties wide latitude in setting social policy, the state government attempted heavy-handed centralized micromanagement. Suppose they decided to basically loot the counties whose social views were out of step with what was fashionable in Sacramento. This would turn their democratic republic into the proverbial three wolves and a sheep voting on what's for dinner.

It is possible to re-draw imaginary lines within a nation without bloodshed? If mankind has not discovered a way to do that, then it is time we learned how. I propose that if a county is adjacent to another co-sovereign to which a super-majority of its citizens wish to join, then it ought to be able to do so. This is provided that the co-sovereign to be joined is agreeable to the transfer, and that no counties in the original state are "cut off" from a state they wish to remain in as a result of the move.

There are some caveats to this. Contracts made under the laws of the old co-sovereign might still be tried in its courts according to its laws. There might be some property of the old co-sovereign within the boundaries of the county which wishes to change sovereigns. There might be some share of state debt which the county would be obligated to pay. It would of course be awkward for politicians who had that county as part of their districts. These issues are resolvable.

There might be one other issue, and that relates to the concentration of wealth. In other words, a rich county in a poor state, but close to a rich one, might want to leave for no other reason than to join with other counties which are as wealthy.

Were such a move easy and inexpensive, over time you would have states which consisted mostly of poor counties which no other state would take. This might lead to concentrations of wealth and poverty not related to the poor decision making of a state government or its inhabitants. There is a moral difference between separating for a just cause and separating for a base one. A wife who leaves her husband because he beats and robs her is not viewed in the same way as one who leaves her husband simply because she found a man with more money.

I suggest a prior agreement whereby an exit fee is paid in certain situations. A county with an average income higher than the state average pays an amount based on the difference of income between itself and the rest of the state which it leaves behind, and also moderated by the wealth of the state which it wishes to join.

As an example, the rule might be that a departing county or region would agree to (in addition to their share of state debt) pay a fee for each voter equal to a seventh part of the annual per person income difference between the area leaving and those left behind, along with a seventh part of the difference between that of the area they will be joining and that which they leave behind.

So if a county with an annual per person income of $50,000 chose to leave a state with an annual per person income of $35,000 to join with a state where the income per person was $45,000 then the exit amount would be ($15,000/7) + ($10,000/7) = $2142.85 + $1428.57 = $3,571.42 per voter.

One may hope that allowing for counties to change sovereigns will be a seldom used power, yet just the existence of this remedy will incentivize a state to treat all of its regions and peoples respectfully.

What of counties in the interior? Some of them will become border counties if others leave. But many will not. It might also be the case that there is no bordering co-sovereign worth fleeing to. Can regions within states have a "when in the course of human events" moment? This is a philosophical question.

There is no reason in principle why they couldn't. A third of California could split off from that state, and still have a greater population than all but seven states. Texas entered the union with an understanding that it could split up into five different states. There are seven U.S. states with a population of less than one million, including some of the best governed in the nation. Seven more have a population of less than two million. It is the largest states which tend to be in the most financial trouble and have the most strife.

In short, a localist philosophy would provide an orderly process within each state, which might vary from state to state, by which localities within the state might exit to join another state willing to accept them. Or if a certain critical mass of localities wished to leave as a group, they might do so and form a new state.

The points I made above about exit fees should the wealthier parts of the state wish to exit from the poorer parts also applies here. That is, wealthy counties trying to form their own state may be obligated to pay an exit fee to the poorer entity they are leaving. Then again, if the wealthier areas feel that the rest of the state is looting them via theft-by-democracy, they might consider the exit fee to be a price worth paying. Why shouldn't they then have the right to pay it and be gone?

Obviously there should be some sort of minimum area and population required to become a new state. Otherwise some cult or crime ring (besides current governments I mean) might get ahold of a single county or two and try to form their own "state". This minimum can be decided in advance so that there is a clear and peaceful path to dissolve political bonds. For the United States the standard might be that a region which wishes to split off and become its own state must be at least as geographically large as the current state with the smallest area, and at least as populous as the current state with the smallest population. In all cases, the areas should be contiguous, and keep counties which wish to remain in the original state contiguous rather than "cut off".

Our Constitution does currently permit these sorts of changes in states and their boundaries, but requires approval of all state legislatures involved, as well as approval of the national government, to do so. From a localist perspective, these restrictions are too onerous. If an entire county, or a dozen counties, feel they are being treated unfairly by the rest of the state, and an adjoining state is willing to take them, why is the permission of those they feel are treating them unfairly required? Why is permission from a distant national government required? Will their decision be more informed than that of those living there? Will it be more just?

So long as there is a procedure for separation, and the financial and other property issues are handled according to procedure, then why should it be so impossible for citizens to peacefully "alter or abolish" their government in this manner?

If a man in a region is unhappy with the politics of a state, his feet can leave the ground. But if all the men of a region are dissatisfied with the politics of a state, their feet may stay, for it will be the ground itself that moves.

It should be built into the national constitution that representatives from a state newly formed by such means will be accorded a place in the national union by default, unless the expulsion measures applicable to all states are applied to the new one.

We would hope that boundaries would rarely change, and that just the knowledge that a disfavored region could leave if provoked enough would cause the remainder of the state to be more responsive to the citizens of that region. Still, it is important that checks and balances be in place to guard against a state becoming, over time, a forced marriage of hostile regional groups with incompatible opinions about how society ought to be ordered and who ought to be obligated to pay the bills for it.

The Seventh Pillar: Citizenship

****

The principle that a sovereign state ought to have the power to determine who its citizens are needs little elaboration, and so I shall not dwell long on it here. Since the 14th amendment, the power to determine citizenship has been taken out of the hands of the states, and even to a great extent out of the hands of the national legislature.

A localist would argue that the national government should retain power to grant federal citizenship only, granting those rights which pertain to the federal citizen (the right to leave a co-sovereign and take their goods with them for example). The states should retain the right to award state citizenship by metrics of their own choosing. Under this system, it could occur that a person (a recent immigrant for example) could be granted federal citizenship who does not have state citizenship. They could vote in federal elections, but not state ones. They would have federal rights, but not the same entitlements as a citizen of the state.

But the importance of this issue is not limited to immigration from other countries, legal and otherwise. A common complaint in smaller states close to California for example, is that "refugees" from California come to their state to escape the mess which results from a particular view of government- but then proceed to vote for that same sort of government in their new home state!

Under localism, a state could protect itself from such an occurrence by lengthening the residency required before new arrivals could vote in state or local elections. They could also attempt innovative solutions to the thorny problem of voters who are tax consumers voting in tax increases over the objections of tax payers.

The bottom line on this issue is that either the state can maintain the power to control who can and cannot be a citizen, or they forfeit that power to another "decider." States denied the power to choose who their own citizens are will become states that are denied the power to choose their own destiny.

Even here in the United States, citizens of states are watching helplessly as Washington enforces a defacto program of generational population replacement to fundamentally alter the political landscape in favor of more government. Even if the existing voters oppose the policy, officials from both parties carry it out.

Why? I would not be surprised if the ruling class finds the American Middle Class to be too uppity and egalitarian-minded for their tastes. This would explain their *de-facto* policy to overwhelm them in the population with large numbers of illegal aliens from nations where the tradition is for the peasants to genuflect before their "betters."

California for example, elected Ronald Reagan as its governor not that long ago. Due to a titanic influx of illegal aliens (who later became citizens or whose children did) from a society more agreeable to larger government, there is simply no way a person with the limited government views of Reagan could be elected to that same office today. Supporters of big government did not wind up running California by winning the argument. They won by replacing the population.

Is it possible such authority will be abused by the states? There is always a chance that power will be abused, even as the Federal government has abused their power. That is why it should be dispersed in the first place! And there are remedies available in a localist nation. Should a state make an abhorrent abuse of such power the proper remedy is expulsion-once all of the federal citizens and localities who wish to separate themselves from such a state have been allowed to do so.

The Conclusion of Things

****

The large central state has but two benefits to the citizen. One of these is simply protection from external threats posed by other large central states. The other is the expanded economic opportunity which comes from free trade and unrestricted travel over wide areas within its borders. There are other benefits to having a government, but these are not dependent on its size.

These benefits, though few in number and oft taken for granted, are not insignificant. Yet with those benefits come a slew of outrages. The military ostensibly used for protection against other nations

The Conclusion of Things

can be turned on its own population. The free trade zones can be subverted into cronyism by unscrupulous business interests who sense that the vastness of the state makes it more profitable to lobby for government intervention than to market to customers for honest trade. Tax policies which make one segment of the population virtual slaves working for the benefit of others cannot be escaped.

Zooming even further back, a central state becomes a magnet for one of the very worst types of human personalities- those who crave power over others. Drawn to the same capitol city, such people will feed off of one another and work day and night to collect more and more power. No doubt the best intentions and motives will be pleaded, but the result will be the same. Their big ideas are built on the loss of our freedom.

A primary goal of localism is to find a way to keep the two advantages of the central state while subjecting government to the discipline of the marketplace. Doing so will naturally put local governments in competition with each other to provide the most freedom at the least cost. Governments which fail to deliver will be both easier to change and easier to flee than a central state which goes awry.

Human government will always be flawed so long as humans themselves are flawed. We need not consider which form of human government is perfect, for none are perfect. Our object here, among those persuaded that government is still necessary, is to maximize the chances that where each person lives they will have the form of government which they feel suits them best. The bar for human government should not be set higher than the bar for man himself!

We need not start from scratch in our considerations concerning a philosophy of government. History has shown mankind glimpses of the best framework for establishing government that flawed humans are capable of devising.

That, in the view of many of us, has taken the form of decentralized confederated constitutional republics established via a compact giving few and defined powers to the central government combined with an open-ended list of which areas of life are individual rights that are off-limits to government intervention.

Such a model has already been devised. Such a model has already been implemented, and such a model has been proven to be successful in providing mankind liberty. The model has been proven, what it has not been, is *preserved*.

Jefferson's observation about the tendency of government to grow and liberty to lose ground proved to be accurate. Each fifty year period of the American Republic from 1776 onwards ended with a central government larger and more intrusive and powerful than the fifty year period before it.

This process continued when the people consented to it, and also when they did not consent to it. It continued when they elected Democrats, and it continued when they elected Republicans. It happened when they elected progressives and when they elected conservatives. It happened despite the checks and the balances erected to prevent it. And this process continued until what we see in American government today is something which no longer resembles the type of government described in the preceding paragraphs.

The checks and balances which the Founders provided in an effort to prevent exactly what has happened were effective in slowing down the process by which liberty is lost, but were ultimately insufficient by themselves. Once local autonomy is lost to any other interest, government policy becomes a true monopoly and the powerful and self-correcting force of the marketplace can no longer be applied to government. Governments no longer have to compete for citizens on any policy question which has been deferred to national authorities.

It is this competition, for business and for citizens, which will force those who run governments to rule with as light a hand and be as small a burden as possible. We do not rely on raising up a better class of elites to foster this outcome. Ordinary fallible men will do this for us. They will do this even if they wish to do otherwise, because the market will punish them if they do not.

As the United States becomes more and more a central autocracy the corrective power of the marketplace is being lost. Poorly run cities use their political clout to get the central government to subsidize them at the expense of those places where government is more competent. Rules are standardized so that instead of being able to move to the next city where the rules are different we more often see that all rules are the same for everyone everywhere. It is increasingly difficult to credibly call this condition of living "freedom."

The loss of freedom and growth/centralization of government may happen "naturally", but it does not happen *inevitably*. It can be stopped, and it can even be reversed. The Leviathan state has not come about by voodoo or magic. It has happened because very clever groups of humans have, acting in their own interests as members of the ruling class of government, used various avenues or pathways to increase the power of the apparatus which they controlled. They practiced various ways to leverage the authority with which they were entrusted into even more authority for themselves. And obviously, the more authority they have over there, with them in the capitol, the less the rest of us have here, where ever we are. What is lost is freedom.

Many of the recommendations in this work take the form of rules or restrictions on behavior. Rules and restrictions are not popular these days. Competing political philosophies offer fewer rules. What they do not offer is a workable solution. They have no means to defend themselves against those who would use freedom in order to destroy it.

To preserve the maximum amount of freedom possible it is necessary to restrict actions by which clever groups of humans have used their own freedom to steal the freedom of their fellow man. Whatever "rules" are in Localism, this is their aim and their purpose- to provide only the minimum restrictions necessary to block centralization of power.

This volume describes thirteen doorways through which power is consolidated, and gives advice on how to close them and keep them closed. The natural tendency of government is to grow. The natural tendency of gravity is to pull a man down to the surface of the earth. Yet we find that despite the presence of gravity, with the judicious application of the principles of aerodynamics men build airplanes and thereby gravity is, if not defeated, at least overcome.

By analogy, the applied principles found in the seven pillars of localism will not change the nature of those who wield power from wanting more of it any more than the lifting shape of a jet's wing stops gravity. Rather, they will *overcome* such tendencies, even as an airplane overcomes the pull of the earth by the use of countervailing physical laws.

The first pillar Localism is built on is a paradox. This is that we can best protect true rights by decentralizing even the power to define rights. Whoever controls the power to define rights controls the whole society, for rights trump even the consent of the governed. If government power must be subjected to the market in order to keep it restrained, then so must the power to define rights, for it is the ultimate government power.

The second pillar is built on a principle much easier to grasp. A federal nation is a union of several co-sovereigns bound together by a pact (the Constitution) which forms yet another entity, the central government. When disputes arise as to the exact meaning of the terms of the compact, each party to it has an equal right to determine what those terms mean.

The idea currently in vogue, that states signed a compact in which only the other party (the central government) could determine what it actually meant, is preposterous. No responsible adult could put their name to such an agreement and whatever the Founders must have meant when they signed the Constitution, it wasn't that! States must have meaningful remedies when they feel that the central government has violated the terms of the compact which binds them together. If they don't, all power eventually winds up in Washington.

The third pillar concerns the role of political parties. Our founders were quite correct to have a formal separation between Executive Branch and Legislative Branch, and between state governments and the central government. But these formal checks, balances, and firewalls can be made without effect if there is an informal system which end-runs them all. Such is a national party system in which the same entity sponsors both Executive and Legislative branch candidates, and both federal and state candidates.

Even worse is that these two national entities are funded largely by corporations, artificial legal persons, whose ownership and scope are global rather than national. Without rules similar to the ones proposed in this work, there is simply no way to keep a political party answerable to the citizens in the heartland.

It might be the third pillar, but in terms of places to start, reforming the political party structure is the first step. This is where the reader can begin to apply the philosophy to life, and can do so today. In most places, it is still possible to go around the party system. What is missing is the understanding in the eyes of the population that a national unitary political party system is a terrible idea which cannot help but undermine the intent of the Founders.

⊹⊱⊰⊹

The fourth pillar, "The Lessons of History" is composed of seven sections, each describing a doorway by which power has been gathered unto one set of hands in one city. The sections or lessons also describe how those doors might be shut. Each lesson is important, even if not all are lengthy. It does not take long to deconstruct how the abuse of the federal judiciary, and the power to regulate commerce, and the construction of trade or environmental treaties, have been used to undermine republican principles. There is little subtlety in the manner in which the federal government has used our own credit to turn the states against us, and used direct taxes to put fear into each of us who has prospered. There is no subtlety at all in the concentration of raw military firepower in the hands of Washington D.C.

Also among the lessons of history is the abuse of corporate "personhood". Our society has been transformed so that artificial constructs of the government are able to accumulate more wealth and get more access to our political system than can real individual persons. A corporation is a collective, one which amplifies the power of those who control it even while it diminishes their accountability. How can leaving such entities with unfettered access to the political system possibly result in a freer or more just nation?

But the biggest lesson of history of all, the central lesson in the central pillar of the philosophy of government called localism, is that which concerns money and banking. No nation with central banking has long maintained a decentralized government. The two concepts of "decentralized government" and "central banking" are mutually exclusive. Those who want the one must give up on the other.

Central banking leads to overall centralization in government, and away from sound money. Much of American history is a struggle against central banking, and if there is one thing history has taught us about money, it is that it is too important to be left in the hands of government.

A sound and just government would protect its people not only from the corrupting influence of its own money, but from the influence of bad money from other governments. A localist nation would not give the national government much authority, but it is essential that it have the authority to protect our economy from the fraudulent fiat currencies of other governments.

The power to issue fiat currency is like the power to control a magic money machine: One which can siphon wealth off from all other units of currency in the world and place that value in the new currency created by the machine. Unless appropriate steps are taken, those who control such a machine will inevitably rule over those who do not.

The fifth pillar of localism is public education. We need diversity of control not just because of what might be taught, but because of what knowledge might be lost. In 1896 William McKinley won a Presidential election and the leading issue was his call to keep the dollar backed by pure gold rather than a mixture of gold and silver as his opponent William Jennings Bryant desired. At that time the population understood the importance of keeping a strong and sound currency. By 1974 all the silver had been removed from our coinage and the dollar was no longer backed by gold anywhere.

Somehow, the basic understanding of economics possessed by the nation had been lost. That is just one example of why the power to decide what the next generation is taught should be left in the hands of local communities rather than decided by a class of "experts" in state or national capitols. Diversity truly is our strength in education in that is makes it harder to convince a population that something false is true, nor can what is once known be as easily forgotten. There should be a marketplace, not a monopoly, as regards to deciding what is worth knowing.

The sixth pillar of localism is that the right of exit for political units should be extended below the state level. Free association of counties should trump imaginary lines on a map. Under previously agreed-to conditions, the citizens of a county ought to be permitted to change states, or in concert with enough other counties, form a new state of their own.

Some of our smallest states are among the best run. Some of our largest states are among the worst run, with internal regions whose inhabitants have a very different view of the world than that of the state as a whole. Why should they be forced together in political union against their will? Does it serve the interests of the average citizen to pretend those bonds are sacred, or that of their rulers?

The seventh pillar of localism is citizenship. No place of liberty can remain so if its population becomes overwhelmed by those who are attracted to the fruits of liberty without an understanding of the basis on which they are obtained. Each state should have the authority to determine on what basis immigrants become citizens. If it is the federal government which has the power to determine when immigrants into a state become state citizens, then those who control the federal government have the power, in the long run, to make that state into whatever they wish it to be. Immigration policy with respect to citizenship must be decentralized.

If a nation leaves open any of those thirteen doorways, the natural tendency of government to grow and liberty to yield ground will assert itself. And government is growing. It is growing at an accelerating pace, despite the wishes of populations around the globe. It is growing despite the rise of philosophies which eschew external government altogether, for such philosophies have no means to defend themselves from the varied means by which freedom is lost as described here.

In the end my friends, I predict there will only be two competing ideas about government: Globalism or Localism. Governments will either continue to consolidate until the ancient dreams of tyrants for a one-world oligarchy come to pass, or else a new dawn of liberty will rise upon the earth.

In such a dawn, the right of the people stated so eloquently in the Declaration of Independence to "alter or abolish" existing forms of government will be exercised and done so peacefully. Some of you reading this work may be among the Founders or Re-Founders of a new and better nation. A nation founded on Localist principles in which each citizen is somebody, and each government will either serve well or perish without bloodshed.

Afterword: On the Superiority of Localism to Libertarianism

"If men were angels, no government would be necessary. If angels were to govern men, neither external nor internal controls on government would be necessary. In framing a government which is to be administered by men over men, the great difficulty lies in this: you must first enable the government to control the governed; and in the next place oblige it to control itself." – James Madison in the Federalist #51

+++

The Libertarian philosophy of government in its various schisms seems to be in vogue at present, and its adherents express a confidence in its virtue all out of proportion to its success at even being implemented, much less producing a place anyone would want to live once it were. Something approximating localism has been done before (early United States history and the Swiss Confederation), and the results have been encouraging.

So far as I know, something approximating libertarianism has not been tried before on a large scale, and we have no actual record against which to compare its promises. The supposed examples I have been given turn out to be much less free of government than advertised (Ireland in the Middle Ages) or small isolated islands where virtually everyone was related. Where libertarian societies have formed on a small scale, they tend to spontaneously collapse after a few years unless they are a small volunteer community within a larger state apparatus.

If one is to evaluate a philosophy of government on its promises rather than what it has been shown to produce when tried, then socialism and even communism have a very strong theoretical case. The nobility of their good intentions is exceeded only by the dreadfulness of their actual track record. I don't have high expectations of a society constructed on the libertarian principle, if one is ever attained.

Not that libertarianism and localism are incompatible on the ground, at least not in the minarchist form of libertarianism. Localism is all about letting people in different localities order their society as they see fit. Should a locality wish to order itself on libertarian ideals, there is no reason why in principle that it could not do so. Localism is not constrained to a certain part of the political spectrum. The rules of society would vary from state to state and even in counties within states to some extent. Enclaves built on ideals from every part of the political spectrum might be contemplated.

Under localism it is moral and economic reality, rather than government force, which will prove which ideas best preserve liberty. The great mass of the philosophy is simply designed to make it easier for individuals to have the government which suits them, and to protect that vital benefit once it is attained.

Libertarians often set up the principle of initiation of force (and most throw in fraud) as the one moral absolute that the state is allowed to punish for. It seems from here to be an effort to cram too much moral reality into too few handy-dandy rules.

A localist would say that people have a right to free association with other like-minded persons, and within that association to order the rules of their society as they see fit, subject to the classical limitations of a Republican form of government with associated individual rights. This too is liberty. This too is being able to live like you want to live, which is a pretty good definition of freedom.

Just as a state might delegate some of its power to the central authority in order to enjoy the mutual advantages of participation in the nation, so a man might agree to mind his personal behavior in order to abide by the wishes of the majority in his city in exchange for the advantages of fellowship with men of similar views.

Let me be very clear though, localism is not communitarianism. The two are actually deadly adversaries. Communitarianism is nothing but cellular fascism. In communitarianism individuals lack rights and must always yield to the view of the entity called the "community". And the communities must have their own will, if a group can even be said to have a will, subordinated to that of the nation.

Localism on the other hand, is all about preventing the concentration of political power in any one place. It thus unleashes the magic of free-market choice to individuals concerning what sort of government they want to live under. Localities are given more power not to submerge the individual, but to empower them.

In localism individuals still exercise the classical rights of a citizen under a Republic. This includes the right to free speech, keeping arms, property rights, due process, equal protection, etc....even if the majority of a given community wishes otherwise.

All the things listed for example under the Bill of Rights can and should be considered individual rights enforceable by the co-sovereign against local government officials even if the community does not wish it. That individual rights exist is not at issue in localism, what is at issue is how expansive a view one can take of what one's "rights" may be.

In the libertarian view, behavior that merely offends others is not eligible for sanction by government. This is not a recipe for a polite society. Rather, it is an invitation for individuals and groups with a grudge against the world, or even against a neighbor, to behave as offensively as possible short of violence.

An enforced Libertarian society would be an invitation for people who crave attention at any cost to invent new ways to shock and offend people. The infamous Westboro Baptist Church would be delighted to relocate to such a community. They could revel in protesting at every child's funeral right in front of the parents, shouting over the mourners about how God struck down their child for their wickedness. They might take great pleasure in calling your girlfriend a whore everyday on the street or in the marketplace. And they would call her a whore, lumping her together with your neighbor who likes to expose himself to children and run naked through the streets with mayonnaise smeared all over his body.

Most people won't live that way. I am not saying that. Most of us are peaceable. But libertarianism most empowers those whose conduct is most offensive to their neighbors. It most empowers those who don't care what their neighbors think and who have little bond with other people. It only takes a small percentage of such people to make life miserable for a lot of people, especially once escalating retaliation for feuds great and small begins.

For the broad mass of people, who live their lives in a peaceable manner, libertarianism is not empowering at all. They rarely do anything that their neighbors would want to sanction by law anyway. For those inoffensive types who keep their minds sound and conduct praiseworthy, and who live among those with habits similar to their own, libertarianism has very little to offer, unless compared to the false choice of a totalitarian dictatorship.

I would suggest that Libertarianism could get as tyrannical as any other system that attempts to impose a uniform moral absolute on a population which by and large does not accept it.

Suppose I and my neighbors felt that the man who likes to run around naked with mayonnaise smeared on his body ought to be sanctioned by law for such behavior. Under a libertarian system it would be authorities from the central government, who do not have to endure the jackass on a regular basis, who would come to our town and order us to cease and desist in the enforcement of our local law because Mr. Mayonnaise did not "initiate force or commit fraud."

I define liberty as the freedom to live as you please. It pleases me to seek out like-minded folks to live around and be able to some extent to legally sanction behavior that is very offensive to the great majority of us.

I am willing to trade some reasonable limits on my public behavior for the advantages of community, so long as I retain the right to vote with my feet if need be. That is how it pleases me to live, and how it pleases most to live. Thus, ironically, libertarianism for most people does not produce the most liberty. It only produces the most liberty for those whose conduct is most offensive to their neighbors. And it has the potential to set up the state as a giant tyranny to make sure that those individuals have maximum liberty at the expense of my own.

But perhaps you are a libertarian who is not persuaded by my rhetoric. You should support localism just the same. Localism is the best shot you will have at getting your libertarian society. Additionally, it is the escape hatch you might need to undo that society should it be less utopian in reality than on paper. Can you imagine trying to undo it under a centralized government where those in the distant capitol, whose whole privileged position is based on their loyalty to enforcing the libertarian absolute, are the last to acknowledge that their theories don't work out?

If libertarianism is correct, in localism it can triumph one locality at a time. Those who wish to flee to it may do so, and if enough wish it they might even bring their cities to you. If it is not correct, or even if it is but some wish not to choose it, then they are free to do so.

This is the moral triumph of localism over not just libertarianism, but all other systems of governance.

What is contained in the localities is up to the people in them, constrained only by the fact that physical, moral, and economic reality will prove some systems unsustainable.

It will not be government force, but natural force and the force of the free market operating in the realm of government that shall determine which philosophies will prevail. The only restrictions are meant to protect the people of communities from ambitious empire builders in distant cities seeking to impose their will on people they don't know. It is an attempt to close every subtle door through which imperial ambitions might creep.

Localism does not *ensure* perfect government, or even good government. No system of government can do that, and the ones which promise it are the sorriest of the lot. It only ensures that people have the government they want and/or deserve. It ensures that a people who want and deserve good government can have it, for in localism power truly is with its safest repository- the people themselves.

THE BEGINNING

Be sure and read the next book on Localism from Mark: "Localism Defended, the Narrow Path Between Anarchy and the Central State".

Also, be on the lookout for Mark's foray into theology with his new book "Early Genesis". Due in late 2016.

13438137R10125

Printed in Poland
by Amazon Fulfillment
Poland Sp. z o.o., Wrocław